The Mythology
of Native
North America

The Mythology
of Native
North America

By David Leeming
and Jake Page

University of Oklahoma Press : Norman

The following myths are reprinted by permission of the publishers: "White Buffalo Woman" (pp. 35–39), "A Gust of Wind" (pp. 43–45), "Coyote, Iktome, and the Rock" (pp. 50–52), "The Man Who Was Afraid of Nothing" (pp. 118–21), "The Ghost Dance at Wounded Knee" (pp. 137–40), "The End of the World" (pp. 140–41), "Little-Man-with-Hair-All-Over" (pp. 168–75), and "The Life and Death of Sweet Medicine" (pp. 179–86), from *American Indian Myths and Legends*, ed. Richard Erdoes and Alfonso Ortiz, copyright © 1984 by Richard Erdoes and Alfonso Ortiz, reprinted by permission of Pantheon Books, a division of Random House, Inc.; "Black Elk Journeys to the Center" (p. 42), from John G. Neihardt, *Black Elk Speaks*, published by the University of Nebraska Press; "First Creator and Lone Man" (pp. 79–84), from Martha Warren Beckwith, *Mandan-Hidatsa Myths and Ceremonies*, Memoirs of the American Folklore Society, copyright © 1938 American Folklore Society and not for further reproduction; "The Setting Out" (pp. 96–99), from N. Scott Momaday, *The Way to Rainy Mountain*, copyright © 1969 by the University of New Mexico; "Ts'its'tsi'nako, Thought-Woman" (pp. 101–2), from Leslie Marmon Silko, *Ceremony*, copyright © 1977 by Leslie Silko, used by permission of Viking Penguin, a division of Penguin Books USA Inc.; "Over the Hill" (pp. 117–18), from Alice Marriott and Carol K. Rachlin, *American Indian Mythology*, copyright © 1968 by Alice Marriott and Carol K. Rachlin, reprinted by permission of HarperCollins Publishers, Inc.

Library of Congress Cataloging-in-Publication Data

Leeming, David Adams, 1937–
   The mythology of native North America / by David Leeming and Jake Page.
   209 p.   cm.
   Includes bibliographical references and index.
     ISBN 0-8061-3012-1 (alk. paper)
   1. Indian mythology—North America. 1. Page, Jake.   II. Title.
   E98.R3L35   1998
   398.2'08997—dc21   97-18451
                                                                    CIP

Text was designed by Alicia Hembekides, set in Garamond with displays in Baker Signet.

The paper in this book meets the guidelines for permanence and durability of the Committee on Production Guidelines for Book Longevity of the Council on Library Resources, Inc. ∞

1   2   3   4   5   6   7   8   9   10

For Pam and Susanne

Contents

Most North Americans have had some experience of mythology by way of translations or the classical texts that have long been a part of the canon of Western literary education. For example, undergraduates and their parents can be expected to have at least some slight visual or literary knowledge of the Greek god Hermes as a messenger of Zeus. For some he would be better known in his Roman form as Mercury, and Zeus would, in that context, be Jupiter. The same readers would probably know that Zeus's wife was Hera, or Juno, and they would remember that Hera had a reputation as something of a nag. Many are aware of the Persephone myth and the Orpheus myth as well, and many with college degrees probably know that Hermes was a trickster and that there was also a Norse trickster called Loki. Some sophisticated students might also be conversant with aspects of Egyptian and even Sumerian mythology, not to mention the stories of the Bible and the great Homeric epics.

But surprisingly few North Americans, even in a graduate class in myth and literature, are able to speak with any knowledge of Coyote, Spider Woman, Glooscap, Water Jar Boy, the many tales of the maiden who fell out of the sky, or what is, in effect, an epic poem called the *Blessingway*. Yet these are characters, events, and works of extraordinary vitality and power that belong to one of the world's richest mythological traditions, which was firmly established in this land when Europeans arrived here several centuries ago. If it is worth our while to be aware of the myths of the ancient Egyptians, Greeks, and northern Europeans, it is just as important for us to be aware of the myths of the land in which we live. It might be said that until we know the ancient collective dreams of what we like to call "our land" and "our nation," we cannot know ourselves or be in any full sense a part of that land.

In any study of mythology certain very real problems must be confronted. A dream belongs to the dreamer; it is a reflection of the individual's experience, and our understanding of it is highly influenced by the way the individual chooses to describe it. In the same way, a myth belongs to a culture with a particular experience and to the storytellers who reveal it. From the very beginning we are several steps removed from the myth and its meaning. This is true, of course, whether we are speaking of Greek myths or Native American myths. It must be stated at the outset, then, in connection with this book and its authors, that few if any non-Indians can convey a full understanding of Native American mythology. Yet dreams and myths are stories created by human beings like ourselves, and all of us, whatever our individual or cultural experiences, share the larger human condition and the need to make sense out of the world around us, our history, and our nature. To avoid discussing Native American mythology, however limited our non-Indian understanding, would be to ignore a significant aspect of the human experience.

It has been argued by many that it is by way of the common threads that we understand each other's experiences, even as we appreciate our individual and cultural differences. The common threads running through American Indian myth and non-Indian myth help us to appreciate the universal human experience in both. To study the Navajo creation myth only as a reflection of Navajo culture is to miss the point that in their myth the Navajos have given us a particular insight into a universal experience. Through the Navajo experience, the Navajo landscape, and the Navajo traditions we understand a bit more about ourselves and creation in general. By the same token, we learn something of our condition by reading *Hamlet*, a play that comes to life in the particular clothes of a medieval Danish society as understood by a Renaissance English storyteller. When we read *Hamlet* we can (with the help of footnotes, to be sure) consider it as a reflection of the Renaissance English experience, but (as several centuries of *Hamlet* observers would testify) the play also, and perhaps more importantly, helps us to better understand what it is to be human. If this were not the case, there would be little reason to recommend the play—or the Navajo creation myth—to those of us who are neither anthropologists nor historians.

What we have done in this book is to choose particular Indian myths that seem to have "literary" appeal and tell them in the context of both the cultural "clothes" through which they take form and the larger community of world mythology and human experience to which they also belong. Coyote and Raven in their story cycles can be recognized as very Indian entities, but they may also be seen as tricksters whose close relatives are such characters as Hermes in Greece, Loki in northern Europe, and Ananse in Africa. Consider the Ojibway vision-quest story of the corn spirit Mondawmin, who dies in order that the tribe of the boy with whom he wrestles may discover corn. We understand that as a collective dream the myth can take on life only in Ojibway terms, but we also relate to it more generally because it speaks to our inner experience of the cost of knowledge and the boons that can derive from struggle. In that respect the Mondawmin myth has relatives in the ancient stories of Osiris and Attis or the somewhat more recent story of Jesus.

It is, of course, true that much is lost in the retelling of these myths. Our sources are Native American storytellers, whose myths have been collected by anthropologists and historians over the years and continue to be collected. These collectors include the artist George Catlin, who visited the Mandan Indians and other Woodland tribes in the early 1830s and studied their myths and rituals; Henry Rowe Schoolcraft, who collected Chippewa (that is, Ojibway) tales at about the same time; James Mooney, who studied Cherokee myths at the turn of the century; the great Franz Boas, who at the same time categorized Native American myths and took note of the common traditions they revealed, opening the way for the work of Stith Thompson, who, under the influence of Antii Aarne, in the late 1920s created a complex motif index for Native American narrative. The many other important contributors to our knowledge of Native American mythologies include Natalie Curtis, Ruth Benedict, Ruth Underhill, John Bierhorst, Lewis Spence, George Bird Grinnell, Frank Hamilton Cushing, Alice Marriott, Carol Rachlin, Richard Erdoes, and Alfonso Ortiz. There are countless Native American storytellers and medicine people who have shared their knowledge with these and other collectors: Black Elk and Leonard Crow Dog, among the Sioux; N. Scott Momaday and Old Lady Horse, among the Kiowa; and Rachel Strange Owl, of the Cheyenne, to mention only a very few.

In some cases we have quoted the storytellers directly; in others we have retold the myths.* Ideally, we would know the languages in which the myths were told and the personalities of the storytellers and medicine people who told them. For obvious reasons the myths are retold here in English, and we have had to accept the stories as they came to us, whatever the personalities, the motives, or the talents of the particular conveyors. There is no pretense here of literal accuracy. Myths are part of an oral tradition and each retelling is slightly different. Sometimes our retellings are attempts to collect what seem to be significant aspects of several versions of given stories. This book, then, is primarily a literary rather than an anthropological exercise. Its purpose is to contribute to the development of the process by which Native American mythology as oral narrative becomes more recognized as an aspect of the overall North American and human experience.

A necessary question arises in connection with any study of a culture's mythology: How do we define myth and, particularly, myth as opposed to folktale? In this book, with very few exceptions, we have chosen as myths stories that speak to such subjects as the origins of the world and life, the forces that control existence, and the struggle of humans to achieve identity and to know their place both in this life and after death. In the broadest sense these are religious subjects, as opposed to the subject matter of folktales, which are meant primarily to entertain. This is not to say, of course, that myths cannot be entertaining. The Native American trickster cycles, for example, are nothing if not entertaining, as are many of the Greek and Roman myths.

What we can say in summary about myth as we use the term here is that a myth is a collective cultural dream through which humans describe, explain, and assimilate the mysteries they experience all around them—in nature, in the cosmos. If we assume a significant role for human consciousness in the overall scheme of things, we might say that in creating myths, humankind has made use of unique mimetic and metaphorical powers to make creation conscious of itself.

DAVID LEEMING AND JAKE PAGE

* The sources for (or other examples of) the retold myths are given after each story. When myths are quoted directly, that is indicated and the source of the quotation is noted.

The Mythology
of Native
North America

Introduction

The Native Americans of North America are people of many languages and many "nations." We have tended to think of them as a single entity primarily because in the invading European's mind, from the 1500s on, an Indian was first an Indian—essentially a subhuman obstacle to the "civilizing" of America—and only secondarily a Hopi, or a Sioux, or an Ojibway. For those Native Americans who survived the invasion, it was necessary, in spite of the establishment of reservations, to learn the ways and the dominant language of the conquerors, often to the detriment of their own lifeways and their own languages. Keeping in mind the need to recognize the cultural differences between the peoples who lived in America before it was "discovered," it can be said that these groups and their descendants did and do have much in common. For instance, although the question is debated by many Native Americans whose traditions and beliefs tell them otherwise, it is generally agreed by historians and archaeologists that the ancestors of all Native Americans came to what we now call America from northeast Asia by way of the ancient land or ice bridge that periodically spanned the Bering Strait. And it can also be demonstrated that sufficient common patterns exist in Indian myths to justify the study of Native American mythology in general as well as the mythologies of particular regions and individual tribes, especially if our focus is primarily literary rather than historical or anthropological. Of course, no literary study of myths can ignore the historical and cultural context in which the stories were told and written down, and the context of Native American mythology is of particular importance in terms of its effect on the narratives themselves.

Archeological evidence suggests the presence of humans in North America in the Paleolithic period. Crude stone tools discovered in what is now Canada, Texas, New Mexico, and California have (very controversially) been dated to about 40,000 B.C.E., and others have been dated, again controversially, to 20,000 B.C.E. It is clear that in about 10,000 B.C.E. a new, much more advanced people with more efficient tools and weapons began to make their way into North America, probably from Beringland and northeast Asia, before the land bridge was submerged as it is now. At any rate, by the time Columbus "discovered" America, the North and South American continents were populated by hundreds of groups of what he called "Indians," thinking at first that he had discovered a new route to India. Some of these cultures—especially the ones in Mesoamerica—rivaled European culture in terms of urban and agricultural development. For example, Tenochtitlan, the Aztec capital taken by Cortez in 1519, was larger, cleaner, better run, and more productive agriculturally than European cities of the time.

Once again it must be said that, as various as Indian cultures had become by the time they moved into North America, they had and have in common an identifiable collective mythological tradition. While each Indian nation's mythology reflects its own cultural experience—its own history, rituals, language, thought patterns, and environment—there are themes and motifs that particularly characterize Native American mythology in general. These common themes, in many cases, can be traced back probably not only to Asian roots but also to the process by which the various people migrated across the continents and, in some cases, changed their basic lifestyles. These similarities go beyond the archetypal patterns that are found in world mythology in general—such patterns as the hero quest or the descent into the underworld. For instance, versions of the earth-diver creation myth, in which an individual dives to primordial depths to bring up material out of which the earth will be made, are found among the Ainu people of Japan, the Altaic people of Mongolia, and various Siberian peoples. Very similar versions can be tracked to Kukulik Island in the Bering Strait, down the West Coast of North America to southern California, and into the Great Plains and the woodlands of the East Coast. Indeed, the earth-diver creation is the dominant creation story (one might even say the dominant myth) of North America; it is told by many Algonquian-speaking (Anishinaubae) peoples as well as the Cherokees, the Iroquois nations, the Mandan, the Osage, the Yakama, and even by the Yuma Indians of Arizona in the single area of the country (the Southwest) where another creation pattern, the emergence story, generally prevails.

The logical assumption is that the diffusion of the earth-diver myth is due to the movement of people from northeast Asia into the Americas. This assumption is strengthened by the frequent existence in the American earth-diver myths of the Asian tendency to associate the creation with trickster-transformers, who in mythologies all over the world embody an elemental, amoral creative impulse. As far as the Southwest's emergence creation story is concerned—a mythic form in which the people move gradually through a series of lower worlds to their present state—it, like the many Indian myths of long treks, is almost certainly a reflection of the process by which hunting-gathering people moved down across North America into Central and South America and then back to the American Southwest, where eventually the agriculturally based pueblos came into being. In short, the emergence myth may well suggest not only the great transcontinental trek but the movement from one kind of culture—that of nomadic hunters and gatherers who settled temporarily as they found wild sustenance—to that of settled agriculturalists.

Various scholars, among them Stith Thompson, Joseph Campbell, John Bierhorst, and researchers for the Smithsonian Institution's *Handbook of North American Indians*, have divided North America into regions and considered the overall pattern of mythological types and motifs as a means of discovering the characteristics of Native American mythology in general and the differences among regions in particular. There are conflicting views regarding the borders of these regions, and they should be considered merely as a working framework. Most would agree to the existence of at least seven areas containing tribal groups whose mythologies form recognizable patterns within the larger pattern. Following this approach, we find several motifs that are emphasized to varying degrees in the different areas, but that form a definite overall Native American pattern. The regions in question are discussed below.

The *Subarctic*, extending from Alaska in the west to Labrador and what is now Maine in the Northeast, includes peoples primarily of the Athabascan language family in the west and Algonquian speakers in the east. They are hunters and fishers, since the climate for the most part makes agriculture impractical. The mythologies of the Subarctic Indians center around an earth-diver creation directed by a supreme being, a myth that in a later form puts more emphasis on a great flood and on the creative work of a culture hero. Shamans and shamanic journeys are important among the northern tribes.

The Inuit ("the Eskimos") are another group of people living in the Far North, in what can be called the Arctic region of North America—which extends from eastern Siberia to eastern Greenland and includes parts of Alaska and northern Canada. Many scholars consider the Inuit to be non-Indian, but their myths reveal a spiritual if not ethnic connection with other Native Americans.

The *Northeast Woodlands*, encompassing the northeast coast of what is now the United States and the area around the Great Lakes, was probably the first temperate area to be entered by the original migrants from Asia. To this day this woodland region is inhabited by three language groups, including Siouan-speakers (such as the Winnebago and Tutelo), Iroquoian peoples (Huron, Seneca, Mohawk, and others), and Algonquians (Southern Ojibway, Menominee, Shawnee, Narraganset, Delaware, and others). The mythology of these peoples is based on a belief in an all-pervasive power, mystery, or "medicine" that exists in the land itself or, more specifically, in such entities as medicine bundles or god figures like the Great Manitou of the

Ojibway, the Delaware (Lenape), and others. Medicine people (some call them shamans)—visionaries trained or born to make particular use of spiritual power—are important for some of these nations, and many of them believe in an earth-diver creation and a supreme creator. Among matrilineal peoples—especially some Iroquoian speakers*—who developed agricultural practices along with their hunting and gathering, there is a myth of edible plants emerging from the dead body of the Earth Mother.

Indians in the *Southeast Woodlands*, in what is now the Deep South of the United States, built burial, effigy, and temple mounds that date back to the so-called Adena, Hopewell, and Mississippian cultures between about 1000 B.C.E. and 1600 C.E. Later the Indians of this region were for the most part Muskogean speakers, but there were also Iroquoian, Siouan, Algonquian, and Caddoan peoples. They were primarily agriculturalists and therefore considerably more sedentary than the peoples of the Far North or even the Northeast Woodlands. Many of these Indians, most notably the Cherokees, were forced to move west during the 1800s. As often is the case with people who live in permanent villages rather than temporary camps, the Southeast Woodlanders developed complex rituals and clan arrangements—in the case of most Southeastern Indians, matrilineal clans. There were medicine people. The cosmos consisted of a world created by an earth-diver—our world, an island on the primeval waters with a stone-vaulted sky hiding a heaven above and an underworld below the waters. This cosmos was controlled by a supreme deity identified with the sun. Rituals of fire were and still are important among the Cherokees and others.

The *Great Plains*, between the Rockies on the west and the Mississippi River on the east, extend from southern Canada to the Gulf of Mexico. The hunting culture here probably developed out of the eastern woodlands as early as 7500 B.C.E., but the picture in the popular mind of Plains Indians on horseback, hunting vast herds of buffalo, is based on a relatively late development, the widespread introduction of the horse by Spaniards in the sixteenth century. Plains

7

Indians also practiced some agriculture and some horticulture, perhaps before the sixteenth century; and they did some sheep herding after the Spanish introduced sheep. But hunting was dominant among the great Plains Indian peoples, who belong to several language groups and whose mythologies are a mixture of traditions from all over North America. The Plains Indians include some of the best-known North American tribes: the Algonquian-speaking Arapaho, Blackfoot, Cheyenne, Cree, and Plains Ojibway; the Athabascan-speaking Lipan and Kiowa Apache, and Sarsi-Blackfoot; the Caddoan-speaking Pawnee and Wichita; the Kiowa-Tanoan-speaking Kiowa; the Siouan-speaking Crow, Osage, Dakota Sioux, Lakota Sioux, Mandan, and Arikara, to mention only some of this most numerous Plains language group; the Tonkawan-speaking Tonkawa; and the Uto-Aztecan-speaking Comanche.

Trickster culture heroes, mediators between the gods and humans, are important on the Great Plains, whether Iktome (Spider), Old Man, Coyote, or the Great Hare. A supreme deity, Wakan Tanka in Siouan, can be loosely translated as the Great Spirit or the Great Mystery. The high god is often the sun, and there is usually an earth-goddess figure such as Mother Corn. There is also a tendency to stress the importance of the hereafter (the "Happy Hunting Ground" in popular usage). Myths associated with the animals of the hunt, like White Buffalo Woman, are common, as are shamans, sacred-pipe myths and rituals, and sun ceremonies.

The *Northwest Coast* extends from southern Alaska south to the Columbia River. The mythologies of the Indians of this region—hunting and fishing people—tend to be localized rather than general. What the tribes have in common are myths having to do with hunted animals and with the relationship between the hunter and his superior prey, which willingly sacrifices itself so that humans may live. Myths of Bear Mother and Salmon Boy are common. Animal totems grew out of intricate clan systems and take material form in crests and in the totem poles unique to the region. Spirits are important in the Pacific Northwest, as well as shamans to regulate or interpret their activities.

Origin myths, reflected in rituals such as the Wakashan Winter Dance, are told to explain how certain ceremonies began. There are few creation stories per se; those that exist are contained in the transformer cycles, stories about the transformer-trickster who does the creator's work by making the world habitable for humans.

California and the Great Basin make up the region encompassing the present state of California and the area between the Sierra Nevada and the Rocky Mountains. The Indians of this region speak a wide variety of languages, and their myths and rituals are extremely varied. There is more uniformity in the Great Basin, where the Numic language family prevails, but this area has always been sparsely populated by Native Americans, and the myth patterns are not always clear. It needs to be said that the Indian cultures of California and the Great Basin suffered greatly at the hands of European and American settlers. First the Spanish missionaries and then American development rendered these tribes marginal and in some cases extinct.

With the coming of Europeans the mythology of the Far West changed. Indications are that before the Christian-influenced supreme deity emerged, the cosmos was directed by a less personal, more mysterious power, perhaps something like the Great Manitou of tribes farther east. Some believe in an earth-diver creation, whose creator is assisted or hindered by a trickster-transformer such as Coyote among the Maidu or Kumokums among the Modoc. Initiatory and world-renewal cults developed around some of these heroes, including the Pomo hero, Kuksu, and Aki and Hesi among the Maidu. There are flood myths among the Salinan, Wiyot, and others; and a *deus faber* (god as craftsman) creation among the Yuki. The Luiseño and the Gabrielino have a dying-god myth and cult, which may well have been influenced by the religion of the European missionaries. The emphasis on a manitoulike power in all things, and on spirits, visions, and dreams, made this region, like so many other Native American culture areas, hospitable to shamanism. As is nearly always the case when individuals are endowed great ritual and mythic power, shamans could become sorcerers as well as healers.

The Southwest, including what is now southern Colorado, New Mexico, southern Utah, and Arizona, was populated by small groups of hunter-gatherers from about 5000 B.C.E. By 1000 B.C.E. there were villages of pit houses; baskets and pottery developed later. Several major cultures grew in this mostly desert region: the Mogollon in the southeast; the Sinagua, Cohonina, Hohokam, and Yuman (Patayan, Hakatay) in the southwest; and the Anasazi in the north. The Mogollon people were the first to raise maize, squash, and beans and are remembered today for their fine Mimbres pottery. The Hohokam were influenced by the Mesoamerican Maya and Aztec peoples in their pottery, their elaborate irrigation practices, and their ceremonial ball courts. The Yuman raised maize and produced brown pottery, but were mostly mobile bands of hunter-gatherers. The Cohonina also were farmers and pottery makers. The Sinagua were builders of pit houses and then pueblos; they also were potters. The best known of these early groups, the Anasazi, progressed comparatively quickly from a maize-growing, basket-making existence in pit houses to become the master builders of the great pueblo structures, kivas, and by 1200 C.E., the cliff dwellings at such sites as Mesa Verde, Canyon de Chelly, and Betatakin. These sites were abandoned by them by around 1300. The Anasazi, like the Hohokam, were influenced by Mesoamerican cultures, particularly in their depictions of animals and religious figures on pottery and their pictographs and petroglyphs on cave and canyon walls.

Descendants of the original southwestern Indians—the Hopi and the Rio Grande Tanoan and Keresan Pueblo peoples in the north, and the Yuma, Pima, and Papago in the south—and Athabascan peoples, the Navajo and the Apache, who came into northern and central parts of the Southwest early in the sixteenth century, form perhaps the richest and most viable concentration of Indian cultures in North America today. The region contains several important cultures. The Athabascan-speaking Navajo, for example, are traditionally sheep herders who live in small family-clan units, although in recent times many have chosen to live in newly created towns. The Hopi, the Zuni, and the Rio Grande peoples are primarily agriculturalists, and they live in the concentrated village settings with which we associate the Spanish word *pueblo*. The Uto-Aztecan, Hokan, Tanoan (Tiwa, Towa, and Tewa), Keresan, and Zunian speakers have a great deal in common—especially in the area of myth and ritual, some of which is likely to have been inherited from Anasazi and Mogollon ancestors. Their rituals and myths influenced the later-arriving Navajo. The Pima, Yuma, and Papago have mythologies that in some cases have more in common with their California neighbors than with the people on the north in the Southwest. Like the Luiseño, for example, the Pima and Yuma peoples have dying-god myths.

As far as the Southwest in general is concerned, it can be said that all of its Native American inhabitants are concerned with rituals that cure sickness, with rituals and myths that bring humans into harmony with nature, with shamanic principles sometimes including witchcraft, and with ceremonies that ensure the success of crops. Naturally, the agriculturalist Pueblo Indians (including Hopi, Zuni, Acoma, and Laguna, as well as the Rio Grande peoples) place more emphasis on agricultural myths and rituals, while the herding Athabascans are more concerned with overall harmony and, like their Asian ancestors, with shamanic cures through the esoteric myths and rituals represented by sand paintings.

The complex rituals and myths of the Pueblo peoples are only partly accessible to outsiders. The Hopi kachina dances and the myths told in the kivas before and after the dances, the Zuni cult systems, the Rio Grande kachina ceremonies, and the clan and religious society practices of all of these peoples are to some extent secret to this day. Even the myths we have are somewhat suspect, as they are not necessarily told to non-Indians with any consistency, perhaps to preserve at least an aspect of secrecy.

Supernatural figures are important among the southwestern peoples. There are personalized gods and goddesses; the Navajo Changing Woman and Spider Woman of the Hopi and other Pueblo tribes are particularly popular. The sun is personified as a male god in most of the region, most especially in connection with the Zuni sun cult. The religious figures best known to visitors to the Southwest are the Hopi kachinas (sometimes spelled *katsinas*); these spirits (depicted in doll-like figures) take material form in the masked dances of particular ceremonies. For the people for whom they dance, the kachinas are in some sense spirits of nature and of the dead. The Hopi say that when they are not in the villages the kachinas live in the San Francisco Peaks (near Flagstaff, Arizona). Somewhat comparable are the Apache *hactin*, who play a significant role in the creation, and the Navajo *yeii*, who are depicted in sand paintings and rugs and appear in rituals as masked dancers.

Without any question, the predominant myth for the people of the Southwest (except for some of the southernmost groups) is the emergence myth, in which, as noted, the people at various stages of their existence move up from a series of lower worlds to the present one. This myth takes several forms, including many oral epics, which often are dominated by culture heroes who undergo trials and quests for the good of the people.

In summary, then, the pattern that emerges in Native American mythology is relatively clear. We have already pointed to the dominance of the earth-diver creation; to the existence, particularly in the Southwest, of the emergence creation; and to the dying-god creation, which is particularly important in California and in far western areas of the Southwest, but also is part of the mythology in other parts of North America. The trickster—the mythological relative of the shamans so important to northeastern Asian and Native American cultures—is present in most regions, usually taking animal form. In the Northwest he tends to be Raven. In the Southwest, the Far West, and sometimes on the plains, he is Coyote. He can be the Spider, Iktome, on the plains. In the Midwest he is the Great Hare. And in the East he is various animals, including Fox, Hare, Turtle, and Badger. Great goddess and high god figures also exist everywhere, as do animal parents and mates, myths of the afterlife and the end of the world, and culture heroes who undergo tests. These heroes (like the shamans to whose rituals they, like the trickster, are mythologically related) travel to the underworld or to the heavens in search of a father, light, fire, or some other boon or deliverance for their people.

These themes and motifs are cultural representations of concerns and experiences that belong to the human race as a whole. Both the earth-diver and emergence creations, although characteristic of the Native Americans in particular, convey the sense that all creation myths do, whatever their type and origin: namely, the sense of birth and differentiation. The shadow myth or archetypal concern behind all particular creation myths is the world culture's collective dream of achieving cosmos out of chaos. In the same way, the descent of Native American heroes to the underworld is meaningful and understandable psychologically for the reasons that people, whatever their religious or ethnic backgrounds, can understand and respond to the descents of Inanna, Theseus, and Jesus to their underworlds. The antics of Coyote and Raven and Iktome are best understood in the context of such figures as the African trickster Ananse and the Norse Loki, and in relation to an aspect of both individual and collective human development.

American Indian myths have been recorded since the first Europeans explored the American continents. As products of oral transmission, these myths, like all myths in preliterate cultures, have continued to develop even as they have sometimes been religiously preserved by storytellers and medicine people. The effect of one tribe's mythology on another because of proximity or trade is evident in many cases too. Even to this day, Indian myths are retold and reworked to fit the realities of present conditions. Different storytellers tell the same stories in various ways. Perhaps most important, Native American cultures have inevitably been affected by the customs and religions—especially Christianity—of the newcomers to North America. For all of these reasons it is difficult, if not impossible, to find the original or "pure" version of an Indian myth, or for that matter, of a Greek, Sumerian, or Egyptian myth. This fact leads us all the more directly to the logic of the so-called comparative approach. In that approach Native American mythology in general—as the sum of its imperfectly perceived individual parts—is seen as an expression of concerns and realities that belong to all of humanity, concerns and realities represented by universal structures such as the descent to the underworld, the essential duality of nature and the universe, the four directions, and the creative-destructive process by which chaos becomes cosmos and returns to chaos.

---

* Matrilineal is not to be confused with matriarchal. In many cultures property descends matrilineally through the female line, giving women a certain importance lacking in patrilineal cultures. In most matrilineal cultures, however, political power remains patriarchally in male hands rather than matriarchally in female hands.

Part One
PANTHEONS

All mythologies of the world are dominated by the concept of divinity. Whatever cultural form the divinity takes—the Great Mother of Sumer, the hawk-headed Horus of Egypt, the bearded patriarch of Jews and Christians, the ox-eyed Hera of the Greeks, or the tree-hanged Odin of the Norse people—these gods and goddesses are considered to be immortal and in a position of supreme power with regard to human beings. In a sense the immortals are a projection of the human dream of a world in which inevitable laws requiring death and disintegration are overcome; something in the universe presents an alternative possibility toward which we can strive. To put it in another way, gods and goddesses are what Mircea Eliade called "fecundators" of the universe. They are the creative force that stands against chaos.

The immortals make things happen; they fill the world with life—not necessarily good life, but life. It is also true, of course, that since cultures clothe the archetype of divinity in their own terms, gods and goddesses are reflections of social realities, value systems, and any given society's view of itself in relation to the cosmos. The Greek Zeus is the top patriarch in a highly patriarchal society, and he does things that a powerful patriarch might be expected to do; he rules arbitrarily, for example, and he is a prideful philanderer. He reflects the Greek world's skeptical view of human nature. The Sumerian Inanna, on the other hand, who descends to a temporary death in the underworld, grew out of an agricultural society that understood and for centuries worshipped female reproductive power and the process

15

by which plants die in the winter and return in the spring. The Egyptian pantheon speaks to the Egyptian culture's preoccupation with death and resurrection and the dominance of the sun. Finally, of course, the immortals often are personifications of aspects of nature and human behavior; there are sun gods, earth goddesses, rain gods, moon goddesses, wind gods, and thunder gods, and there are gods and goddesses of war, of wisdom, of love.

Perhaps the most important role of deities is to provide us with a sense of significance in a universe that otherwise might be seen as random in nature. The existence of gods suggests that we have meaning, and given our consciousness and our ability to use language and to create powerful art and ritual, it suggests that we might be the collective mouthpiece of creation. Thus we see ourselves as made "in the image of God" or as the guardians or namers of creation. Philosopher Raimundo Pannikar says that deity is the metaphor for "man's effort to discover his identity in confrontation with the limits of his universe" (Eliade, *Encyclopedia* 4:264). The god archetype is based in our hope of a relationship between a significant cosmos and our inner being.

Native American Deities

The American Indian concept of divinity begins with a belief in a supernatural world or a spirit power—*manitou* in the woodlands and *wakan* among Plains Indians, to name two instances. The power is manifest in nearly everything in this world. The supernatural world can be invoked for particular purposes through intricate ceremonials directed by priests, medicine people, or shamans and through the sheer physical arrangements of human space. The spirit world is invoked by the Hopi Indians, for example, in the kachina dances and in the symbolic architecture of the kiva, the underground religious structure in which there are clan altars and a *sipapu*, or small hole representing the door by which, in the emergence myth, the people came into this world. The traditional Navajo home—the hogan—is arranged, with the door facing east, in such a way as to represent the world as described in the creation myth of the Blessingway ceremony—a world suffused by the spirit world. Iroquois longhouses and most other traditional Indian dwellings are also arranged symbolically. By this arrangement harmony between our world and the other is maintained.

The deities who inhabit the spirit world are of various types, depending on the particular tribe. In most cases there is a supreme being, a god who sometimes is a personification of the sky or, especially in the western half of the North American continent, of the sun. Usually this supreme god—the Great Spirit, the Great Mystery, Father Sky, Old Man, Earthmaker, or one of several other names—is the prime creator. Sometimes he is assisted by a goddess consort in what can be called a world-parent myth in which the father is sky and the mother is earth. Sometimes he is assisted or hindered by a trickster-transformer or a dying god. Native American culture tends to be more concerned with the earthly effects of divinity than with philosophic theology, and it is the goddess, the trickster, and the dying god, along with culture heroes, who more often than not interact directly with the people, rather than the aloof sky god, much as Jesus and Dionysus rather than God and Zeus interact with their people. In some cases, especially when the culture is matrilineal, the goddess—Spider Woman, Changing Woman, White Buffalo Woman—is in effect, if not in theory, the most important divinity. She or the trickster plays the crucial role of telling the people how to live—that is, how to survive both physically and spiritually.

Also prevalent in the other world are spirit figures who enter this world—often through complex ceremonies—to bring favors, divine knowledge, and a proper balance of the natural elements. Hopi kachinas dance to bring rain, Apache *hactins* help with the creation, Eskimo *inuas* are pantheistically in all aspects of creation and make possible various transformations important to Eskimo

17

mythology. Individuals and clans can have particular guardian spirits or totems, as well, and myths often speak to this fact through stories of vision quests that result in significant and mysterious contact between the seeker and the spirit world. Many of the vision-quest stories include ritualistic spirit journeys of shamans to the other world. It is also clear that shamanic rituals, so important to Native American culture, may in turn influence the myths of culture heroes, especially those who travel to the sky or to the spirit world below.

The World Parents

Among the myths of American Indians we find an occasional treatment of the world-parent archetype. This tradition often involves the separation of primordial earth and sky deities so that creation can take place between them. In Egypt Geb (earth) and Nut (sky) are separated for this reason. In Togo the Krachi people tell how Wularbi (heaven—male) lived on top of Asase Ya (earth—female) until humankind, who had little room to move between them, tickled Wularbi so much that he left Asase and went up above. Earth and sky, or the primordial waters and sky—symbols of female and male— when locked together represent total equilibrium or, in the context of creation, total nondifferentiation. Only through their separation can creative differentiation, or life as we know it, take place.

The world-parent separation is more often than not a reflection of an animistic understanding of nature in which the world is directly formed from the primordial parent or parents. In ancient Sumer the god Marduk made the world and the sky out of the slain primordial parent, the goddess Tiamat. The Aztecs had a similar myth about the goddess Coatlicue, who was ripped in two to form earth and sky.

Among the North American Indians the world-parent myth is fairly rare. It exists most clearly in the religions of the Luiseño and

Diegueño Indians of southern California, and somewhat more questionably in that of the Zuni of New Mexico.

In the Diegueño story there is little of the violence usually associated with the world-parent separation motif, but there is a definite separation, suggesting the need for differentiation between earth and sky before creation can take place.

Diegueño: Tu-chai-pai Makes the World

When Tu-chai-pai made the world, the earth was a woman and the sky a man. At that time the earth was only a lake covered with bulrushes, and the sky came down over the earth and weighed heavily on it. Between earth and sky Tu-chai-pai and his young brother Yo-ko-mat-is were cramped.

Tu-chai-pai took some tobacco in his hands, rubbed it until it was fine, and blew on it three times. Each time he blew, the sky rose up. Then the brother tried this, and each time the sky rose a little farther up. Together they did it and the sky rose all the way up.

Then the two brothers drew the lines on the earth that made the four directions. Knowing that people would come from the four directions, Tu-chai-pai made the hills and valleys and small lakes, since they would need water to drink. He made forests to provide them with wood.

The world was ready, so Tu-chai-pai took some mud and made people—first the Indians, then the Mexicans. It took a long time to make women—they were harder to fashion. He told the people they need never die, but must keep walking. He did give them sleep so they wouldn't have to walk in the dark. The world was dark at that time, and Tu-chai-pai told the people to walk to the east, to the light.

When they reached the light they were very happy. Tu-chai-pai told his brother to make the moon, and told the people that when the moon grew small and might die, they must run races. Tu-chai-pai watched them do this. He was then finished with his creating, and did no more, but he continued thinking for a long time.

(Leeming and Leeming, *Creation* 68–69; Erdoes and Ortiz 156–57
from DuBois)

19

The Luiseño myth is more violent. The world parents are brother and sister—not surprising in these myths, since the two primal parents come from the same source—and creation comes about when the brother assaults the sister.

Luiseño: How the World Was Made

In the beginning was the space-void, Kevish Atakvish.

Things began to fall into forms.
Time came. The Milky Way.
There was no light yet, only a creative stirring.

Kevish Atakvish made a man, Tukmit, the sky, and his sister, Tomaiyovit, the earth. They could not see each other but they coupled and conceived and gave birth to the first things of the creation—valleys, mountains, stones, streams, all the things needed for worship and ceremonies and cooking.

And from the earth came forth the terrifying meteor and its son, the immortal soul of humans. Wiyot came forth also at this time, and from Wiyot came the people.

It was dark and the Earth Mother made a sun, but it was too bright. It frightened the people and had to be hidden. More people came forth from Wiyot and they followed the growing earth as it stretched to the south. Then, at a place called Temecula, the Earth Mother brought out the sun again. The people raised it up to the sky and it began to follow a regular path, and it wasn't so frightening anymore.

(Leeming and Page, God 68; Leeming and Leeming, Creation 243–44;
Leach 60–63; Weigle 202–205)

The world-parent myth usually involves creation through sexual contact. In the Zuni myth as reported by Frank H. Cushing in the late 1800s there is such contact between the parents, Father Sky and Mother Earth, but later versions of the Zuni creation tend to ignore this aspect, casting some doubt on the validity of Cushing's sources. The myth that follows, however, has become a part of the Native American canon. It is one aspect of a complex emergence creation and ritual cycle that has to do with the dualities of chaos and order, being and nonbeing, and it includes the ritual separation of earth and sky and the resulting creation between them.

Zuni: Earth Mother and Sky Father

In the fourfold womb of the world, all terrestrial life was conceived from the lying together of Earth Mother and Sky Father upon the world waters. Earth Mother grew large with so great a number of progeny. She pushed Sky Father away from her and began to sink into the world waters, fearing that evil might befall her offspring, just as mothers always fear for their firstborn before they come forth.

Unnerved by this foreboding, she kept her offspring unborn within her and discussed her fears with Sky Father. Together, they wondered how, even in the light of the sun, these offspring would know one place from another. Changeable as are all surpassing beings, like smoke in the breeze, the couple took the form of a man and a woman.

Suddenly a great bowl filled with water appeared nearby and Earth Mother realized that each place in the world would be surrounded by mountains like the rim of the bowl. She spat in the water and, as foam formed, she said, "Look, it is from my bosom that they will find sustenance."

She blew her warm breath over the foam, and some lifted, sending down mist and spray in great abundance. "So," she said. "Just so will clouds form at the rim of the world where the great waters are and be borne by the breath of the surpassing beings until your cold breath makes them shed downward—the waters of life falling downward into my lap where our children will nestle and thrive, finding warmth in spite of your coldness."

In this way, and many others, Earth Mother and Sky Father provided for their progeny, the people and the other creatures of the world.

(Leeming and Page, *God* 120–21; Sproul 284–86 from Cushing)

The Great Goddess

While the world-parent myths tend to emphasize the dualities and the struggle between earth and sky—the warm, nurturing female principle and the cold male principle—there are mythologies that eschew these issues in favor of a dominant goddess or a dominant god, essentially separate from a mate.

In parts of the late Upper Paleolithic world (c. 10,000–7000 B.C.E.), the hunting-and-gathering lifestyle was tempered by, and in some cases replaced by, agriculture and animal husbandry and consequently stable settlements or villages, where such crafts as pottery and weaving were extensively practiced, and where religious ideas and rituals could be firmly established. It seems clear from ruins, figurines, and other artifacts—especially in the warmer areas of Europe, the Middle East, and the Indian subcontinent—that goddess religion was important if not the dominant cult. As birth givers women were logically associated with the fruit-bearing earth, and it was natural to see the earth itself as a great mother. There were many Great Mother earth goddesses after the early Neolithic period (c. 6500 B.C.E.) in the ancient world. We know them in forms that they perhaps assumed still later: Inanna, in Sumer; Devi, in India; Astarte, in Phoenicia; Hathor, in Egypt; and Gaia, in Greece. Eventually these goddesses were all superseded by male sky-war gods in the patriarchy that came with the development of war and various new technologies, but even in their subdued state, goddesses remained important as guardians of agriculture, home crafts, and childbirth.

The great-goddess archetype is firmly established in Native American mythology. As in all parts of the world, the archetype takes many striking forms, but essentially it is nearly always a nurturing earth mother. The goddess is perhaps most important in the Pueblo cultures of the Southwest, the communities of the Southeastern Indians, and parts of the Northeast that, to a great extent because of climate, developed agricultural–animal husbandry and craft economies. However, there are goddesses of great importance in all Native American cosmologies—some associated with particular crops or animals, and a few associated with the sun. Some of the importance of the American Indian goddesses must be attributed to the matrilineal systems of so many tribes.

An example of the goddess in her ancient animistic form as earth itself is the Okanagon Earth Mother. The Okanagon, a Salishan-speaking people of the northwestern United States, came to see the creation in a Christian light, with a male creator, but this myth suggests an earlier belief in a primal mother creation.

Okanagon: The Mother of Everyone

The old one made earth from a woman. She was to be the mother of everyone. So the earth was formerly a human being and lives still, but transformed so we cannot see her as the person she is.

But she still has the parts of a person—legs, arms, flesh, and bone. Her flesh is the soil; her hair is the trees and other plants. Her bones are the rocks, and her breath is the wind. She lies, her limbs and body extended, and on her body we live. When it is cold, she shivers; when it is hot, she sweats.

And when she moves, there is an earthquake.

(Leeming and Page, *Goddess* 12; Sproul 243 from Teit)

Although in most cases of sun worship the sun is personified as a male, a significant number of sun goddesses exist. The Arunta people of Australia worship Sun Woman, and the major Japanese deity is the sun goddess Amaterasu. An important American Indian example of a sun goddess is the Cherokee Grandmother Sun, whose story, told below, has parallels in other tales of a god or goddess whose disappearance because of the loss of a child brings pain to humankind. Such a story was that of the Hittite god Telepinu, who had to be coaxed out of his cave in order that the earth might become fertile again, or that of the Greek Demeter and her daughter, Persephone, whose annual return from Hades brings life back to the earth. The Cherokee myth also is reminiscent of the Orpheus myth, in which the hero travels to the underworld to retrieve his dead wife; and the story of Grandmother Sun also has a flood myth attached to it. Its emphasis on the sun is in keeping with the Cherokee worship of fire. It is said that it was Spider Grandmother who stole fire for the people.

Cherokee: Grandmother Sun

The sun's daughter lived in a house in the sky directly above the earth, and every day, when the sun made her journey from the other side of the vault of the sky, she would visit her daughter. Once there, the old woman often complained about her grandchildren, the people of the earth. They never would look directly at her, she said; instead they would only screw up their faces and squint at her briefly.

The moon, however, found the people, his younger brothers, to be handsome, since they often smiled up at him in the night sky. It did not take long before the sun was deeply jealous of the moon and his great popularity, and she decided to kill the people. Sitting in her daughter's house one day, she refused to leave and instead sent down a killing heat. Many people died, and the rest despaired. Desperate, they sought help from some friendly spirits called Little Men.

The Little Men thought and said that the only way the people could save themselves was to kill the sun herself. They changed two of the people into snakes and sent them up into the sky to wait until the sun went to dinner. Then, it was planned, they would leap out from their hiding place and bite her.

When the time came, one of the snakes—an adder—was blinded by the sun's light and could do nothing but spit out yellow slime. The sun called him a nasty name and flounced back into the house. The other snake—a copperhead—was so put off at this that he gave up altogether and crawled away.

24

Meanwhile, people continued to die from the searing heat of the angry sun, and they pleaded again with the Little Men for help. Again they transformed two of the men—one into a fierce horned monster, and the other into a rattlesnake. Most people placed their bets on the monster, and the rattlesnake, not to be outdone, raced ahead and coiled himself up on the doorstep of the sun's daughter's house. When the daughter opened the door and called out for her mother, the rattlesnake struck and killed her. So excited was he that he forgot all about the old sun and returned to the people, followed by the disgusted horned monster. The monster continued to be furious, growing so difficult that the people had to banish him to the distant end of the world.

Meanwhile, the sun found her daughter dead and, in grief, she shut herself up in her house. The world turned dark, and the people realized they had to coax the sun back out of the house or they would all perish in the cold, not the heat. The Little Men explained that their only hope was to bring the sun's daughter back from the country of the ghosts in the Darkening Land in the west. For this mission they chose seven men and gave them a box to carry, as well as a wooden rod each, along with some precise instructions.

Before long, the seven men arrived in the Darkening Land and found a huge crowd of ghosts dancing, and there, in the outer circle of dancing ghosts, was the sun's daughter. As she went past, one of the men struck her with his rod. Each man in turn did the same, and after the seventh man had struck her, she fell out of the ring and was promptly put in the box. Meanwhile the other ghosts danced on without noticing.

As the men headed eastward, the daughter inside repeatedly asked to be let out. She was cramped. She was hungry. She was smothering. As the men neared home, they began to grow anxious that she might really be dying in the box, so they opened the lid just a crack and something flitted past them with a fluttering sound. Then, from the bushes nearby, they heard the singing of the redbird. They shut the lid of the box and proceeded, only to discover when they reached home that the box was empty.

(Because they let the daughter of the sun escape—and she now sings for all the people in the form of the redbird—it has been impossible since that time to bring back people who die.)

The sun had been full of hope that she would see her daughter again but, realizing that she would not, she wept and wept, causing a great flood on the earth. Now the people were in danger of drowning. So they sent a number of their handsomest young men and their most beautiful young women up into the sky to dance, in hopes of distracting the sun. In her grief, the sun was not to be deterred, and wept on. Finally, the dancers told the drummer to play a different song, and they danced to the new one, and the sun looked up. The new music and the young people were so beautiful that the old sun gave up her grieving and once again smiled.

(Leeming and Page, *Goddess* 57; Erdoes and Ortiz 152
from Mooney, *Cherokee*)

Several goddesses play significant roles among the Pueblo people of the Southwest. As agriculturalists, the Pueblos' concern has understandably been the productivity of the earth and the cycles on which this productivity depends. The seasons are reflected in the annual cycle of ceremonies that characterizes all of the Pueblo peoples and in their myths of the sun and especially of goddesses. The Hopis have several important goddesses, reflecting their matrilineal system. There is Hahaiwuuti, mother of the kachinas, who is particularly associated with the care of Palulukong, the female Horned Water Serpent. Tiikuywuuti (Child-Water Woman) is another Hopi deity associated with fertility. Among the best known of Hopi goddesses is Huruingwuuti (Hard Substances [or Hard Beings] Woman), who is not unlike Sus'sistinako (Thinking Woman) of the Keres pueblos in that her cosmic responsibility is material things. The most important Hopi goddess, however, is Kokyanwuuti (Spider Woman or Spider Grandmother), who is a major figure in the tribe's emergence creation story. She taught the people weaving, among other things, but she can also, like the spider, be dangerous. Spider Woman plays a role in many Native American mythologies—the Zuni, the Navajo, the Pueblo, the Pawnee, and the Cherokee, to mention only a few. The myths that follow reveal two of the many sides of this most popular of Native American goddesses. The first is a Hopi myth revealing Spider Woman's central place in the process of creation.

Hopi: Spider Grandmother Leads the People

In the beginning there was endless space, in which nothing existed but Tawa, the sun spirit, who contrived to gather some of the elements of space and inject some of his own substance into them and thereby create the First World, inhabited by insectlike creatures who lived in caves and fought among themselves. Dissatisfied, Tawa sent a new spirit, Spider Grandmother, down to prepare them for a long trip. She led them on a long journey during which they changed form, grew fur on their bodies, acquired tails, and took on the shape of dogs, wolves, and bears.

They arrived in the Second World, but Tawa was still displeased because these creatures did not understand the meaning of life any more than their predecessors had. So Spider Grandmother was dispatched again, and while she led them on their second journey Tawa created a Third World, lighter and moist. By the time they arrived in the Third World, they had become people. Spider Grandmother cautioned them to renounce evil and live in harmony.

They built villages and planted corn, but it was cold. Again Spider Grandmother arrived; she taught them to weave and make pots. But the pots could not be baked, and the corn did not grow well because of the chill.

One day a hummingbird arrived, explaining that he had been sent by Masauwu, who lived in yet another world above the sky, called the Upper World. Masauwu was the owner of fire and the caretaker of the place of the dead. The hummingbird taught the people to make fire with a drill. Then he left.

They learned to bake their pottery so it wouldn't break. They warmed their fields by lighting fires. They cooked their meat instead of eating it raw. Things were better in the Third World now.

But soon sorcerers began to unleash evil into the world, making medicines that would harm people and turn their minds from virtue. Men gambled instead of tending their fields. Women revolted. Rains failed to come, and the corn failed.

Spider Grandmother came again to warn them, telling the people who still had good hearts that they should leave this world and go to the Upper World. A chief and his wise men prayed for four days and then, out of clay and by performing a special ceremony, they created a swallow and asked it to find a way to the Upper World. The swallow flew high up into the sky and found an opening, but strong winds buffeted it and it flew back.

The chief and the wise men made a dove, and it flew through the opening and found a great land spreading in all directions but with no life on it. The dove flew back and reported.

This time the men made a hawk, and it flew up, only to return with the same message. Finally, a catbird flew through the opening and came upon Masauwu, who said the people could come. Hearing this message, the people were elated. Then they realized they had no way to climb up to the opening. Spider Grandmother reminded them of the chipmunk, who lived on pine nuts and might help them plant a tall tree.

They enlisted Chipmunk. He planted a spruce, but it didn't grow tall enough. Then he tried a fir pine, but it grew only slightly higher. A long-needle pine also failed. The chipmunk asked if someone with an evil heart was present, and all the people assured him of their pure intentions. The fourth time, a bamboo reed was tried, and Spider Grandmother told the people to sing so it would grow high. Eventually, it succeeded in growing through the opening. This was the sipapuni, and Chipmunk explained that the people could climb up through it because it was hollow.

The chief and the wise men drew four lines in the ground and said if any sorcerers crossed the lines they would perish. Then, led by Spider Grandmother and her twin sons, the people climbed up the reed into the upper world—the present Fourth World of the Hopi.

(Page and Page, *Hopi* 152–54; Waters 4–8; Courlander 17–26)

Another Spider Woman myth is the Cherokee version of the theft of sun and fire.

Cherokee: Spider Grandmother Brings Fire to the People

In the beginning there was no light whatsoever. Everyone kept bumping into one another and, after groping blindly around like this, they said the world needed light. Fox explained that he had heard of some people on the other side of the world who had some light, but they were greedy people and would not share it with anyone.

Possum said that he would go and steal it, hiding it in his bushy tail, and bring it back. So off he went to the other side of the world and found the sun hanging in a tree. He went over to the sun and snatched a piece of its light and put it into his bushy tail. But the light was so hot that it set his tail on fire and burned off all the fur. The greedy people there saw this and took back the light for themselves, leaving Possum with his bald tail.

Hearing this, Buzzard said he would try, and instead of hiding the light in his tail, he would put it on his head. That was his plan. He flew over to the other side of the world, dove straight into the sun, and grabbed it in his talons. He put it on his head, and it promptly burned the feathers off, leaving him with a bald head to this day. The people there saw this too, and snatched the sun away from him.

Meanwhile, people were still bumping into each other because it was dark, and Spider Grandmother said she would try to help them. She spun a web that reached all the way to the other side of the world, where it was light. She was so small that none of the greedy people saw her coming along the web. Quickly she grabbed the sun and put it in a bowl of clay. Then she raced back home with it along a strand of her web, and the world now was light and the people rejoiced.

Along with the sun, Spider Grandmother brought fire and soon taught the Cherokee to make pottery too.

(Erdoes and Ortiz 154–56 from Mooney, *Cherokee*)

A goddess whom some scholars see as a version of Spider Woman is Sus'sistinako (Thinking Woman, or sometimes Tsityostinako, Prophesying Woman, or Tsichtinako), who is the primary creatrix of the Keres pueblos in New Mexico (Acoma, Laguna, Santa Ana, Zia, San Felipe, Santo Domingo, and Cochiti), though at some pueblos, such as Zia, Spider is a male. Thinking Woman is an example of a creator who made forms out of her thoughts. The creator of the Mariana Islands in the South Pacific works the same way, as do the much-less-personalized Indian concept of Brahman and the Hebrew God of Genesis. There are creation-by-thought myths among several other Native American tribes, including the Arapaho, the Omaha, the Pomo, the Winnebago, and the Zuñi.

In the Zia male Spider myth, there is, as Hamilton Tyler notes, a sense of a priest performing a ritual chant, a "thinking outward into space." Although at Zia the principal figure is male rather than female, the elements of the myth are the same as when it is told at the other Keres pueblos on the Rio Grande.

Zia: Spider Sings the World

In the beginning there was only Sus'sistinako, a spider. In that time there were no other animals, birds, reptiles, or other living things but the spider.

Spider drew a line of meal north to south and another east to west, making a cross, and placed two small parcels north of the crossline, one to the east and one to the west. These precious parcels contained the seeds of the twin mothers who bore humankind and all other living creatures, but no one knows just what these seeds were—no one but Sus-sistinako.

After putting the parcels in place, Sus-sistinako sat down on the west side of the north-south line and sang. Before long the two parcels began to quiver in time with low sweet music, like rattles. After a while two women appeared, one from each parcel, and soon people, birds, and the other creatures began to appear and walk about on the earth, and Sus-sistinako kept singing until the creation was complete.

(Tyler 91–92 from Stevenson)

Thinking Woman is generally thought to have produced two daughters from her place under the earth. These daughters, in terms of the metaphor involved, play the role of seed-bearing plants in relation to Thinking Woman as Corn Goddess, who sends up her power from the earth, of which she is the personification. In this Acoma myth Thinking Woman is Tsichtinako, and her daughters are Iatiku (Bringer of Life) and Nautsiti (Full Basket).

Acoma: Tsichtinako and Her Daughters

In the beginning two sister-spirits were born underground in the dark, where they grew slowly and knew each other only by touch. Tsichtinako fed them and taught them language.

When the right time arrived, she gave them baskets containing seeds along with models of the animals that would be in the next world. The seeds and models were, Tsichtinako said, from their father, and the sisters were to carry them into the light in the next world. She helped the sisters find the seeds of four trees in their baskets, and they planted them in the dark. After a very long time, the seeds sprouted and one seedling, a pine, eventually grew tall enough to break a small hole through the earth above, letting in some light.

With Tsichtinako's help, the sisters found the model of Badger and gave it the gift of life. They instructed Badger to dig around the hole to make it bigger, but they cautioned him not to enter the world of light. He obeyed, and as a reward the sisters promised him happiness in the upper world. Next they found the model of Locust in the baskets and breathed life into him. "Go smooth the edges of that hole," they instructed, "but don't go through it into the world of light."

31

When Locust was finished, he returned to the sister-spirits. They questioned him, and finally Locust admitted that he had gone through the hole into the world of light.

"What was it like up there?" the sisters asked.

"Flat," Locust said.

The sisters finally agreed that Locust could come with them into that world, but for being disobedient he would have to live in the ground and die and be reborn each year.

It was now time for the sisters to emerge into the next world, but they needed to learn some things first. Tsichtinako came to them and told them about the four directions and that the sun would appear from the east. She taught them some prayers to the sun and a song they could sing, and when they had learned these things, she told them to take their baskets, and Badger and Locust, and climb the pine tree. From its highest branches, they broke through into the world. They repeated the prayer to the sun that they had learned, and sang the song—the song of creation—and stood waiting for the sun to appear in the east.

While they waited, Tsichtinako told them that she had been sent to act as their constant guide in this world, which the creator, Uchtsiti, had made from a clot of blood. It was the sisters' task to complete the creation, she told them, and this they could do by breathing life into the seeds and models in their baskets.

The sun rose in the east, and the sisters planted their seeds and breathed life into the animals. Then it grew dark. The sisters were terrified, but Tsichtinako explained that they could sleep when it was dark, and that the sun would come again the next day. And so it was.

Before long, the creation was complete and the sisters took the names Iatiku (Life Bringer) and Nautsiti (Full Basket). There are stories about what happened to the sisters after that. Some say they quarreled and were deserted by Tsichtinako. Others say that Nautsiti disobeyed her father and gave birth to two sons, sired by hot drops from the rainbow, and that is why Tsichtinako deserted them. It is also said that one of the boys was raised by his aunt, Iatiku, and married her when he grew up, and that together they made the people. It is also said that Iatiku later created the kachinas, the spirits who spend part of the year in the sacred mountains and part of the year dancing to bring rain.

(Leeming and Leeming: *Creation* 3–4; Weigle 215–18;
Erdoes and Ortiz 97–105 from Forde)

Among the Navajo the primary goddess is Estsanatlehi (Changing Woman), who, among many other things, is a miraculous birth giver, in the manner of the Aztec mother of Quetzalcoatl and so many other mothers of culture heroes. Her children are the twins, Monster Slayer and Born for Water, who made the world safe for the Navajo people.

Changing Woman has similarities to the Keres Iatiku, the Pawnee Moon Woman (who provided her people with corn and the buffalo for sustenance), and the Apache White Painted Woman, who, like Changing Woman, is made pregnant by the sun and, in keeping with the Athabascan tendency to mythologize in dualities, sometimes has an evil and opposite sister. Changing Woman possesses the bundle of creation, whose powers are embodied in her. She plays a dominant role in Navajo myth and ritual, including the female puberty rite, or Kinaalda, so important to the Navajos (and the Apaches)—a four-day ceremony during which a girl becomes a woman and, on the final day, gains the healing power of Changing Woman herself.

Changing Woman was found in the form of a small, perfect turquoise female by First Man during a great storm on Giant Spruce Mountain (today known as Gobernador's Knob, in northwestern New Mexico). First Man and First Woman raised her to adulthood there.

Navajo: Changing Woman and the First Kinaalda

When Changing Woman gave sign that she had achieved her first menses, it was seen as a great and propitious occasion by First Man and First Woman. They began a four-day ceremony and celebration. First Woman, in the role of Ideal Woman, assisted her by adorning her with the finest jewels and beads: jet, coral, turquoise, and obsidian. She dressed her in a magnificent woven white dress, with moccasins and leggings. Corn of many colors was gathered, and Ideal Woman brushed her hair, thus combining thought and life and value: what the Navajos call hozho, or beauty.

Each day of the four-day ceremony, the girl-goddess ran to the east toward the sun, farther each day toward beauty. In the course of the ceremony, Ideal Woman massaged her, from head to toe, into the strength and power of womanhood. She had, then, the capacity to bear children—the twins who would one day render the world safe for the people.

Such an event, such a ceremony, is not likely to be forgotten and is commemorated in the songs that accompany Kinaalda today, as in this fragment:

> Now the child of Changing Woman, the sounds have returned,
> Turquoise Girl, the sounds have returned,
> The child of the west, the sounds have returned,
> Her turquoise shoes, the sounds have returned,
> Her turquoise leggings, the sounds have returned,
> Her turquoise clothes, the sounds have returned,
> Now, a perfect turquoise having been placed on her head, the sounds
>   have returned,
> Her turquoise head plume, the sounds have returned,
> Now at its tip there are small blue female birds, truly beautiful:
> it is shining at its tip, the sounds have returned,
> They call as they are playing; their voices are beautiful,
> the sounds have returned.

> (Page and Page, Navajo 152–53)

A Plains Indian version of much of what is contained in Changing Woman is the story of the Sioux provider goddess, White Buffalo Woman, who brought the Calf Pipe ritual that is central to Sioux religious practices. This is the myth as told by the Sioux medicine man John Fire Lame Deer.

Sioux: White Buffalo Woman

One summer so long ago that nobody knows how long, the Oceti-Shakowin, the seven sacred council fires of the Lakota Oyate, the nation, came together and camped. The sun shone all the time, but there was no game and the people were starving. Every day they sent Scouts to look for game, but the scouts found nothing.

Among the bands assembled were the Itazipcho, the Without-Bows, who had their own camp circle under their chief, Standing Hollow Horn. Early one morning the chief sent two of his young men to hunt for game. They went on foot, because at that time the Sioux didn't yet have horses. They searched everywhere but could find nothing. Seeing a high hill, they decided to climb it in order to look over the whole country. Halfway up, they saw something coming toward them from far off, but the figure was floating instead of walking. From this they knew that the person was wakan, holy.

At first they could make out only a small moving speck and had to squint to see that it was a human form. But as it came nearer, they realized that it was a beautiful young woman, more beautiful than any they had ever seen, with two round, red dots of face paint on her cheeks. She wore a wonderful white buckskin outfit, tanned until it shone a long way in the sun. It was embroidered with sacred and marvellous designs of porcupine quill, in radiant colors no ordinary woman could have made. This wakan stranger was Ptesan-Wi, White Buffalo Woman. In her hands she carried a large bundle and a fan of sage leaves. She wore her blue-black hair loose except for a strand at the left side, which was tied up with buffalo fur. Her eyes shone dark and sparkling, with great power in them.

The two young men looked at her open-mouthed. One was overawed, but the other desired her body and stretched his hand out to touch her. This woman was lila wakan, very sacred, and could not be treated with disrespect. Lightning instantly struck the brash young man and burned him up, so that only a small heap of blackened bones was left. Or some say that he was suddenly covered by a cloud, and within it he was eaten up by snakes that left only his skeleton, just as a man can be eaten up by lust.

To the other scout who had behaved rightly, the White Buffalo woman said: "Good things I am bringing, something holy to your nation. A message I carry for your people from the buffalo nation. Go back to the camp and tell the people to prepare for my arrival. Tell your chief to put up a medicine lodge with twenty-four poles. Let it be made holy for my coming."

This young hunter returned to the camp. He told the chief, he told the people, what the sacred woman had commanded. The chief told the eyapaha, the crier, and the crier went through the camp circle calling: "Someone sacred is coming. A holy woman approaches. Make all things ready for her." So the people put up the big medicine tipi and waited. After four days they saw the White Buffalo Woman approaching, carrying her bundle before her. Her wonderful white buckskin dress shone from afar. The chief, Standing Hollow Horn, invited her to enter the medicine lodge. She went in and circled the interior sunwise. The chief addressed her respectfully, saying: "Sister, we are glad you have come to instruct us."

She told him what she wanted done. In the center of the tipi they were to put up an owanka wakan, a sacred altar, made of red earth, with a buffalo skull and a three-stick rack for a holy thing she was bringing. They did what she directed, and she traced a design with her finger on the smoothed earth of the altar. She showed them how to do all this, then circled the lodge again sunwise. Halting before the chief, she now opened the bundle. The holy thing it contained was the chanunpa, the sacred pipe. She held it out to the people and let them look at it. She was grasping the stem with her right hand and the bowl with her left, and thus the pipe has been held ever since.

Again the chief spoke, saying: "Sister, we are glad. We have had no meat for some time. All we can give you is water." They dipped some wacanga, sweet grass, into a skin bag of water and gave it to her, and to this day the people dip sweet grass or an eagle wing in water and sprinkle it on a person to be purified.

The White Buffalo Woman showed the people how to use the pipe. She filled it with chan-shash, red willow-bark tobacco. She walked around the lodge four times after the manner of Anpetu-Wi, the great sun. This represented the circle without end, the sacred hoop, the road of life. The woman placed a dry buffalo chip on the fire and lit the pipe with it. This was peta-owihankeshni, the fire without end, the flame to be passed on from generation to generation. She told them that the smoke rising from the bowl was Tunkashila's breath, the living breath of the great Grandfather Mystery.

The White Buffalo Woman showed the people the right way to pray, the right words and the right gestures. She taught them how to sing the pipe-filling song and how to lift the pipe up to the sky toward Grandfather and down toward Grandmother Earth to Unci and then to the four directions of the universe.

"With this holy pipe" she said "you will walk like a living prayer. With your feet resting upon the earth and the pipestem reaching into the sky, your body forms a living bridge between the Sacred Beneath and the Sacred Above. Wakan Tanka smiles upon us because now we are as one: earth sky, all living things, the two-legged the four-legged, the winged ones, the trees, the grasses. Together with the people they are all related, one family. The pipe holds them all together.

"Look at this bowl" said the White Buffalo Woman. "Its stone represents the buffalo but also the flesh and blood of the red man. The buffalo represents the universe and the four directions because he stands on four legs for the four ages of creation. The buffalo was put in the west by Wakan Tanka at the making of the world to hold back the waters. Every year he loses one hair and in every one of the four ages he loses a leg. The sacred hoop will end when all the hair and legs of the great buffalo are gone and the water comes back to cover the Earth.

The wooden stem of this chanunpa stands for all that grows on the earth. Twelve feathers hanging from where the stem—the backbone—joins the bow—the skull—are from Wanblee Galeshka, the spotted eagle, the very sacred bird who is the Great Spirit's messenger and the wisest of all living ones. You are joined to all things of the universe for they all cry out to Tunkashila. Look at the bowl: engraved in it are seven circles of various sizes. They stand for the seven sacred ceremonies you will practice with this pipe and for the Ocheti Shakowin, the seven sacred campfires of our Lakota nation."

The White Buffalo Woman then spoke to the women telling them that it was the work of their hands and the fruit of their bodies which kept the people alive. "You are from the mother earth," she told them. "What you are doing is as great as what the warriors do."

And therefore the sacred pipe is also something that binds men and women together in a circle of love. It is the one holy object in the making of which both men and women have a hand. The men carve the bowl and make the stem; the women decorate it with bands of colored porcupine quills. When a man takes a wife, they both hold the pipe at the same time and red trade cloth is wound around their hands thus tying them together for life.

The White Buffalo Woman had many things for her Lakota sisters in her sacred womb bag—corn, wasna (pemmican), wild turnip. She taught them how to make the hearth fire. She filled a buffalo paunch with cold water and dropped a red-hot stone into it. "This way you shall cook the corn and the meat," she told them.

The White Buffalo Woman also talked to the children, because they have an understanding beyond their years. She told them that what their fathers and mothers did was for them, that their parents could remember being little once, and that they, the children, would grow up to have little ones of their own. She told them: "You are the coming generation, that's why you are the most important and precious ones. Some day you will hold this pipe and smoke it. Some day you will pray with it."

She spoke once more to all the people: "The pipe is alive; it is a red being showing you a red life and a red road. And this is the first ceremony for which you will use the pipe. You will use it to keep the soul of a dead person, because through it you can talk to Wakan Tanka, the Great Mystery Spirit. The day a human dies is always a sacred day. The day when the soul is released to the Great Spirit is another. Four women will become sacred on such a day. They will be the ones to cut the sacred tree—the can-wakan—for the sun dance."

She told the Lakota that they were the purest among the tribes, and for that reason Tunkashila had bestowed upon them the holy chanunpa. They had been chosen to take care of it for all the Indian people on this turtle continent.

She spoke one last time to Standing Hollow Horn, the chief, saying, "Remember: this pipe is very sacred. Respect it and it will take you to the end of the road. The four ages of creation are in me; I am the four ages. I will come to see you in every generation cycle. I shall come back to you."

The sacred woman then took leave of the people, saying: "Toksha ake wacinyanktin ktelo—I shall see you again."

The people saw her walking off in the same direction from which she had come, outlined against the red ball of the setting sun. As she went, she stopped and rolled over four times. The first time, she turned into a black buffalo; the second into a brown one, the third into a red one; and finally, the fourth time she rolled over, she turned into a white female buffalo calf. A white buffalo is the most sacred living thing you could ever encounter.

The White Buffalo Woman disappeared over the horizon. Sometime she might come back. As soon as she had vanished, buffalo in great herds appeared, allowing themselves to be killed so that the people might survive. And from that day on, our relations, the buffalo, furnished the people with everything they needed—meat for food, skins for their clothes and tipis, bones for their many tools.

(Quoted from Lame Deer in Erdoes and Ortiz 48–52)

The central Inuit Oqomuit tell of the goddess Sedna, whose painful but creative existence reflects the harshness of their own lives and a highly dualistic view of nature. Inuit means "the people" and is derived from *inua*, the word for "soul." The Inuit are Arctic Native Americans but, technically speaking, not American Indians, yet their dominant goddess myth is of interest in the context of Native American mythology in general.

Oqomuit: Sedna and Anguta

At one time Anguta lived with his daughter Sedna, a beautiful and greatly desired young woman. One spring day a great seabird, a fulmar, flew over and urged her to follow him to his home over the sea. Intrigued, Sedna followed, but when she arrived at the fulmar's home, she was horrified by his foul tent and lack of food. In despair she called for her father, Anguta, and after a year he did come with the warm winds that break up the ice. He killed the fulmar and put Sedna in his boat for the journey home.

The other fulmars soon found the body of their chief and mourned—as they still do today with their sad voices—and grew angry. They searched the sea for the murderer, and when they spied Anguta's boat, they blew up a huge storm. Overtaken, the boat was thrown about by the surging seas, and Anguta, to save himself, threw his daughter Sedna overboard. When in desperation she reached for the boat, her father chopped off her fingers. Some of her fingers sank and became whales; others became fish and various sea creatures. Finally Sedna herself sank into the depths and the storm subsided. But she was not dead. She swam up again and climbed into the boat.

Of course, she no longer loved her father, and when he was asleep, she ordered her dogs to bite off his hands and feet, which they promptly did. When Anguta woke up and saw what had happened to him, he flew into a rage and cursed everything and everyone, and the earth swallowed him, and the dogs, and Sedna. Just as Sedna disappeared, she created deer.

Now, Sedna, her dogs, and her father live under the world in a place called Adlivun. Sedna rules; Anguta hobbles about, footless; and when people die they go to Sedna's house in Adlivun. The bad ones have to sleep with Anguta, who pinches them.

(Leeming and Leeming, *Creation* 217–18; Leach 47–50)

The Supreme God

Even in cultures where the Great Goddess has been all-powerful, the male high god has played an important role as a seed bearer to the female principle. And as the goddess power gave way to the demands of more warlike and more technological cultures in the Neolithic period in the Fertile Crescent, southern Europe, the Indian subcontinent, and elsewhere, the highest priorities of nearly all of the world were embodied in a high god who was the most powerful of beings and also the primary creator of the universe. There were, of course, exceptions to this rule, especially among peoples that were matrilineal, as were many of the Native American tribes. And there were and still are Indian peoples, such as several of the Algonquian tribes, for whom the high god, the Kitchi Manitou, or Great Mystery, is neither male nor female. But generally speaking, the male high god who sits in judgment over humanity from his position in the heavens has been the center of the world's religious systems for at least some five thousand years; that is, for as long as patriarchy has been the basis of social arrangements. This is the father god archetype that took the form of the Babylonian Marduk, who rid the world of the female primordial power, Tiamat; or the world creator and judge who is Yahweh; or the god of thunderbolts who is Zeus or Thor. The father god is the deity made in the image of a human being, the image of a male-dominated, power-dominated value system that has been basic to human society in historical times. The very word *god* in most languages summons up the image of a patriarch.

The Native Americans, like most peoples, have their male deities, and even in the mythologies of matrilineal cultures there tend to be creator–sky gods who, in theory at least, are rulers of the universe, even if they also tend to leave most of the arrangements to earth goddesses or trickster-transformer assistants. In fact, such an arrangement is an accurate representation of social arrangements even within matrilineal cultures, in which the female perhaps owns the house she and her husband live in and controls the distribution of plant seeds, but is subservient to the male in politics and religious ceremonies.

More often than not, Native American father gods, like those of many cultures—the Egyptians and the Aztecs, for example—personify the sun. The sun god is typically the fecundator of the female earth. Usually it is said that the sun leaves his house in the east each morning, and, traditionally, the people pray to him. He is also often worshipped in song, and dwellings are built to face and welcome his rising. During the day he passes across the sky to his western house. His path is analogous to the true path each individual hopes for in his or her life. The sun nourishes the people with his warmth, but given his great power, he can also be dangerous and punishing to his children. Some tribes, such as the Oglala Sioux, have elaborate rituals honoring the sun god. Among the Sioux the high god, usually described with the male pronoun, is Wakan Tanka (the Great Spirit or Great Mystery), who, according to the medicine man Black Elk, is at the center of everything that is. In a vision Black Elk journeyed to the center, and from there, basking in the truth of the Great Spirit, he could see and know all things.

Sioux: Black Elk Journeys to the Center

I was still on my bay horse, and once more I felt the riders of the west, the north, the east, and the south, behind me in formation, and we were going east. Then I was standing on the highest mountain of them all, and round about beneath me was the whole hoop of the world. And while I stood there I saw more than I can tell and I understood more than I saw; for I was seeing in a sacred manner the shapes of all things in the spirit, and the shapes of all shapes as they must live together in one being. And I saw the sacred hoop of my people was one of many hoops that made one circle, wide as daylight and as starlight, and in the center grew one mighty flowering tree to shelter all the children of one mother and one father. And I saw that it was holy.

(Quoted from Black Elk in Neihardt)

The sun god, Tawa, is the original Hopi creator. He resembles many creators in world mythology in that he exists alone in the primal void and creates by thought.

Hopi: Tawa and Sotuknang

In the endless space there was only Tawa, the creator. There was no beginning, no end, no time, no shape, no life. Only a void that had its beginning, end, time, shape, and life in the mind of Tawa.

Then he, being infinite, created the finite, the first being, his nephew Sotuknang, whom he ordered to carry out Tawa's plan for life.

Sotuknang gathered out of endless space what would become solid substance and molded it into shapes and forms. Then he went to Tawa, asking, "Is this according to your plan?"

Tawa pronounced it very good and sent Sotuknang back to work. This time Sotuknang gathered from endless space what would become the waters and placed them on the solid surfaces so that the world was half solid and half water. Again, Tawa pronounced the work well done, and sent Sotuknang back to work.

From endless space, Sotuknang gathered all the elements that would become the air, made them into great forces, and arranged them into gentle ordered movements. Again, Tawa was pleased. And again, Tawa sent Sotuknang back to work, this time to create life for this new world of solid substance, water, and air. So out of endless space, Sotuknang created Spider Grandmother to help him in this task.

(Waters 3–4)

The father god as the sun is frequently the agent of miraculous conceptions, as we have seen in connection with the Navajo Changing Woman and the Apache White Painted Woman. The Ojibway, or Chippewa, Indians of Minnesota in the Northeast Woodlands are an Algonquian people who have traditionally harvested wild rice, which has made them dependent, like all agriculturalists, on not only the earth but also the sun. This is a myth involving the sun god Geesis, who takes advantage of a gust of wind to send sacred twins into the world. It is told by David Red Bird, a Green Bay Ojibway singer-storyteller.

Ojibway: A Gust of Wind

Before there was a man, two women, an old one and her daughter, were the only humans on earth. The old woman had not needed a man in order to conceive. Ahki, the earth, also was like a woman—female—but

43

not as she is now, because trees and many animals had not yet been made.

Well, the young woman, the daughter, took her basket out one day to go berrying. She had gathered enough and was returning home when a sudden gust of wind lifted her buckskin dress up high, baring her body. Geesis, the sun, shone on that spot for a short moment and entered the body of the young woman, though she hardly noticed it. She was aware of the gust of wind but paid no attention.

Time passed. The young woman said to the old one: "I don't know what's wrong with me, but something is." More time passed. The young woman's belly grew bigger, and she said: "Something is moving inside me. What can it be?"

"When you were going berrying did you meet anyone?" The old woman asked.

"I met nobody. The only thing that happened was a big gust of wind which lifted my buckskin dress. The sun was shining."

The old woman said "I think you're going to have a child. Geesis, the sun, is the only one who could have done it, so you will be the mother of a sun child."

The young woman gave birth to two boys, both manitos, supernaturals. They were the first human males on this earth—Geesis's sons, sons of the sun.

The young mother made cradleboards and put the twins in these, hanging them up or carrying them on her back, but never letting the babies touch the earth. Why didn't she? Did the Old Woman tell her not to? Nobody knows. If she had put the cradleboards on the ground, the babies would have walked upright from the moment of their birth, like deer babies. But because their mother would not let them touch earth for some months, it now takes human babies a year or so to walk. It was that young woman's fault.

One of the twins was Stone Boy, a rock. He said: "Put me in the fire and heat me up until I glow red hot." They did, and he said "Now pour cold water over me." They did this also. That was the first sweat bath. The other boy, named Wene-boozhoo, looked like all human boys. He became mighty and could do anything; he even talked to the animals and gave them their names.

(Quoted from David Red Bird in Erdoes and Ortiz 150–51)

All high gods are not personifications of the sun. The Iroquoian Hi'nun in this somewhat rarely told version of myth is a thunder god who, like Zeus in relation to the Titans or the Babylonian Marduk to Tiamat, is the destroyer of primordial monsters who once dominated the world. Monster slaying, as we shall see later in our discussion of hero myths, is as popular in Native American mythology as it is in most other traditions. It is noteworthy that the principal monster defeated by the male god here is, as so often is the case in world mythology, a female water serpent, like the Babylonian Tiamat or the Canaanite Lotan or the biblical Leviathan. It is as if, in the patriarchy, the clarity and warlike qualities of the sky god must conquer the mysteries of the depths.

Iroquoian: Hi'nun and the Water Serpent

Rain poured down and thunder rumbled, and a hunter—Hi'nun—took refuge under a great tree in the forest. Beyond the sound of the thunder, he became aware of a voice urging him to follow, and he felt that he was slowly rising from the earth. Before long he was in the sky, gazing downward.

The hunter was surrounded by what seemed to be men led by a chief. The men asked the hunter to look down to the earth and tell them if he saw a huge water serpent, but he could not. Then the chief anointed the hunter's eyes with a sacred salve so that he could see in the watery depths beneath the earth the shape of a dragonlike serpent.

"Kill it," the chief commanded one of the men, and this warrior loosed arrow after arrow at the serpent, but to no avail.

The chief than asked the hunter to kill the serpent monster below. Drawing his bow, the hunter took careful aim, and the arrow sped into the depths where it was lost to sight. But there arose a great din below, the great serpent leaping and writhing in the bloodstained waters. So great was

45

the din that the heavenly beings who accompanied the hunter themselves trembled. But gradually the great din subsided, and the mortally wounded serpent sank under the water's surface. The waters grew calm and finally there was peace.

The chief said his thanks to the hunter, who was led back to earth. It was in this way that humankind first came into contact with Hi'nun, the power who would protect the people from unfriendly forces of the world.

(Spence 218–19 from Erminnie Smith)

Other Deity Types

Other deities that appear in Native American myths include the trickster and the dying god or goddess, as well as lesser deities.

The Trickster

The trickster is probably one of the earliest forms of the more general god archetype. Joseph Campbell called the trickster "the chief mythological character of the Paleolithic world" (*Masks* 1: 273). Carl Jung saw the trickster as the expression of a "preconscious" creative state, and it can be argued that the trickster's activities—often dangerous and antisocial—were later "civilized" or channeled to good purpose in shamanic rituals and activities and in the miraculous activities of culture heroes who can even die, travel to the underworld, and return to life. Among the Pueblo peoples in the American Southwest, for example, the trickster evolved ritualistically into clowns (Koshare, Koyemshi, Newekwe) who display the open sexuality and gluttony associated with tricksters, but are confined within ritual ceremonies and therefore rendered less dangerous. It can also be argued that both tricksters and shamans are related to the mythic and ritual forms associated with the Animal Master, the powerful animal—the bear, the buffalo, the deer, even the salmon—cast in the role of protector and enabler of the hunt (see the Bear Man–dying-god myths, below). An example of this shaman–Animal Master–trickster combination may well exist in the most ancient of art forms—the cave paintings, like the famous sorcerer painting in Les Trois Frères Cave in France, which dates to about 14,000 B.C.E. In that depiction we have what appears to be a dancing human, dressed in an animal costume, with the typically phallic aspect of the trickster.

The trickster is particularly popular in northeastern Asia, Africa, and North America, but he also is present in characters such as Loki in northern Europe, Hermes in Greece, and Reynard the fox in European folklore. The trickster, regardless of the cultural form, tends to express unbridled human desires. He is highly sexed (like the Anasazi Kokopelli, the hunchbacked flute player and possible trickster, he is frequently depicted ithyphallically). He is excessively demanding of food. And he is totally amoral in pursuit of what he wants (rather like Freud's portrayal of the normal baby). Yet the phallicism, the emphasis on excrement and genitalia, and the over-whelming desires are representative of the trickster's essential creativity. It is the trickster's urges and his denial of boundaries that frequently make him a useful assistant to the world creator, and sometimes he is the sole creator. The point is, his desires and his pursuit of them are thoroughly human; the trickster works in our world, not in heaven. This is so even though he has superhuman powers of transformation. He can—like Jesus, the Hindu Krishna, or Buddha, who all possess certain trickster-transformer-shamanistic aspects—transcend human limitations. He can change his shape, and he can move between the worlds here, above, and below.

No region in the world, with the possible exception of Africa, is so trickster-oriented as Native North America. Most tribes have tricksters just as most have the institution of shamanism and the myths of the trickster-descended culture hero. Tribes that survive by hunting emphasize rituals and myths of the trickster-related Animal Master. In most cases the Native American tricksters appear in their prehuman animal forms, though they can be mistaken as humans. The best-known Indian tricksters are probably Coyote, Raven, the

Great Hare, and Spider. These animals appear in the mythologies of many groups and have various tribal names. There are also Indian tricksters who may be said to be transitional between the pure trickster state and that of the more controlled culture hero. These figures, among many Algonquian tribes, for example, are generally not liars or gluttons; they stand for the values of the given cultures and for particular understandings of human nature. Examples are Manabozho, or Nana'b'oozoo (sometimes also Winabojo or Nanabush), of the eastern woodlands, the Algonquian Glooscap, and the Great Hare of the Plains Indians.

Many trickster myths form story cycles. Sometimes these cycles and the stories they contain seem to be less myths than folktales intended primarily for entertainment. Yet the moral and religious importance of trickster myths and cycles cannot be ignored. It has been argued that the funny and immoral activities of the trickster are used to teach children morality by negative example. But the most important function of the Native American trickster in general is to mediate between the human world and the divine, to call attention to the element of disorder—even death—that makes the world real and alive, and like the earth goddesses of some mythologies, to teach humans how to survive. It must be noted, too, that the trickster does play amoral or immoral tricks and that sometimes he is the butt of his own antics.

Easily the favorite among North American tricksters is Coyote. Coyote crosses tribal boundaries with as much ease as he crosses moral and social ones. He exists in the West from Alaska to the great deserts, he is everywhere on the Great Plains, and he ranges even to the East Coast. Sometimes he "hangs out" with other tricksters, such as the wily Plains trickster Iktome (Spider). Coyote is lecherous beyond belief; he is a thief of food, goods, virginity, and the wives of others. He is always creative—sometimes positively, sometimes only in his own interest. He can take many shapes; that is, he is a transformer, not only as an assistant to the creator but as a master of disguise.

In this myth of the Maidu Indians in California, Coyote seems to have brought mischief into a perfect world. In fact, he brings tears and death—that is, he brings uniquely human emotions and the reality of the end of life, without which there cannot be human life as we know it.

Maidu: Coyote and the Footrace

In the beginning, when there was only night and water, a raft brought two persons—Turtle and Earth Initiate. Working together, they created first some dry land, then the sun and the moon and the stars, as well as a large tree with many kinds of acorns. Before long, Coyote and his pet, Rattlesnake, emerged of their own accord, and Coyote watched with great interest as Earth Initiate fashioned all the animals from clay. He watched with even keener interest when Earth Initiate created First Man and First Woman.

Coyote thought it looked pretty easy, so he tried to make some people himself, but they didn't work out because he laughed while he was making them. Earth Initiate said, "I told you not to laugh," and Coyote told the world's first lie, saying that he hadn't laughed.

Earth Initiate wanted life to be easy and full for the people, so every night he saw to it that their baskets were filled with food for the next day. No one had to work; no one got sick. One day he told the people to go to a nearby lake, and he explained to First Man that by the time he got there, he would be old.

Sure enough, when the people reached the lake, First Man was white-haired and bent. He fell into the lake, which shook, and the ground underneath roared, and soon he came to the top, a young man again. Earth Initiate explained to all the people that when they got old, all they needed was to plunge into the lake and they would be young again.

Then one day, Coyote visited the people and they told him how easy life was, how all they needed to do was eat and sleep.

"I can show you something better than that," Coyote said, and he told them he thought it would be better if people got sick and died. The people had no idea what he was talking about, so he suggested that they begin by having a footrace. He told them to line up to start the race.

At this moment his pet, Rattlesnake, went out along the race course and hid in a hole with just his head sticking up. Then the race began.

Some of the people were faster than others and began to pull ahead from the pack, and one in particular ran fastest. This was Coyote's son, and Coyote, watching from the sidelines, cheered him on with pride. But then his son came to the hole and Rattlesnake raised his head and bit him on the ankle. The boy, Coyote's son, fell over and within moments was dead.

The people all thought the boy was too ashamed to get up, but Coyote explained that he was dead. Coyote wept—the first tears—and he gathered up his son and put him in the lake, where the body floated for four days without reviving. So Coyote dug a grave and buried his son and told the people that this was what they would have to do from then on.

(Leeming and Page, *God* 52–53; Thompson, *Tales* from Dixon)

A more typical Coyote myth is this White River Sioux tale in which Coyote's defeat serves as a moral lesson. The story, told by storyteller Jenny Leading Cloud on the Rosebud Reservation in South Dakota, bears some resemblance to cartoons as the flattened-out trickster, like Bugs Bunny, can miraculously unflatten himself at will.

Sioux: Coyote, Iktome, and the Rock

Coyote was walking with his friend Iktome. Along their path stood Iya the rock. This was not just any rock; it was special. It had those spidery lines of green moss all over it, the kind that tell a story. Iya had power.

Coyote said: "Why, this is a nice-looking rock. I think it has power." Coyote took off the thick blanket he was wearing and put it on the rock. "Here, Iya, take this as a present. Take this blanket, friend rock, to keep you from freezing. You must feel cold."

"Wow, a giveaway!" said Iktome. "You sure are in a giving mood today,

"Ah, it's nothing. I'm always giving things away. Iya looks real nice in my blanket.'

"His blanket, now," said Iktome.

The two friends went on. Pretty soon a cold rain started. The rain turned to hail. The hail turned to slush. Coyote and Iktome took refuge in a cave, which was cold and wet. Iktome was all right; he had his thick buffalo robe. Coyote had only his shirt, and he was shivering. He was freezing. His teeth were chattering.

"Kola, friend of mine," Coyote said to Iktome, "go back and get me my fine blanket. I need it, and that rock has no use for it. He's been getting along without a blanket for ages. Hurry; I'm freezing!"

Iktome went back to Iya, saying: "Can I have that blanket back, please?"

The rock said: "No, I like it. What is given is given."

Iktome returned and told Coyote: "He won't give it back."

"That no-good, ungrateful rock!" said Coyote. "Has he paid for the blanket? Has he worked for it? I'll go get it myself."

"Friend," said Iktome, "Tunka, Iya, the rock—there's a lot of power there! Maybe you should let him keep it."

"Are you crazy? This is an expensive blanket of many colors and great thickness. I'll go talk to him."

Coyote went back and told Iya: "Hey, rock! What's the meaning of this? What do you need a blanket for? Let me have it back right now!"

"No." said the rock. "what is given is given."

"You're a bad rock! Don't you care that I'm freezing to death? That I'll catch a cold?" Coyote jerked the blanket away from Iya and put it on. "So there; that's the end of it."

"By no means the end," said the rock.

Coyote went back to the cave. The rain and hail stopped and the sun came out again, so Coyote and Iktome sat before the cave, sunning themselves, eating pemmican and fry-bread and wojapi, berry soup. After eating, they took out their pipes and had a smoke.

All of a sudden Iktome said: "What's that noise?"

"What noise? I don't hear anything."

"A crashing, a rumble far off."

"Yes, friend, I hear it now."

"Friend Coyote, it's getting stronger and nearer, like thunder or an earthquake."

"It is rather strong and loud. I wonder what it can be."

"I have a pretty good idea, friend," said Iktome.

Then they saw the great rock. It was Iya, rolling, thundering, crashing upon them.

"Friend, let's run for it!" cried Iktome; "Iya means to kill us!"

The two ran as fast as they could while the rock rolled after them, coming closer and closer.

"Friend, let's swim the river. The rock is so heavy, he sure can't swim!" cried Iktome. So they swam the river, but Iya, the great rock, also swam over the river as if he had been made of wood.

"Friend, into the timber, among the big trees," cried Coyote. "That big rock surely can't get through this thick forest." They ran among the trees, but the huge Iya came rolling along after them, shivering and splintering the big pines to pieces, left and right.

The two came out onto the flats. "Oh! Oh!" cried Iktome, Spider Man. "Friend Coyote, this is really not my quarrel. I just remembered, I have pressing business to attend to. So long!" Iktome rolled himself into a tiny ball and became a spider. He disappeared into a mousehole.

Coyote ran on and on, the big rock thundering close at his heels. Then Iya, the big rock, rolled right over Coyote, flattening him out altogether

Iya took the blanket and rolled back to his own place, saying: "So there!

A wasichu rancher riding along saw Coyote lying there all flattened out. "What a nice rug!" said the rancher, picking Coyote up, and he took the rug home.

The rancher put Coyote right in front of his fireplace. Whenever Coyote is killed, he can make himself come to life again, but it took him the whole night to puff himself up into his usual shape. In the morning the rancher's wife told her husband: "I just saw your rug running away."

Friends, hear this: always be generous in heart. If you have something to give, give it forever.

Quoted from Jenny Leading Cloud in Erdoes and Ortiz 337–39)

A story told by the Brule Sioux, perhaps as a warning to young girls, illustrates the creativity of the trickster in pursuit of his lascivious needs.

Sioux: Iktome Tricks the Maiden

Iktome's eye had been caught by an especially beautiful young woman, whose ignorance of the ways of men and women was as evident as her virginity. He longed to sample this fresh fruit, and so he dressed himself in the clothes of a woman and sought her out, finding her on the edge of a stream, preparing to cross it.

"Let's wade across together, my young friend," Iktome said in the quavering voice of an old woman.

The girl smiled and they lifted up their robes and stepped into the water.

"Your legs," the girl said. "They're very hairy."

Iktome sighed. "Yes, it happens with age."

As the water grew deeper, they hiked up their robes a bit farther, and the girl tittered. "You backside is hairy too," she said.

"Yes, it happens to some of us older people."

The water grew still deeper, and when Iktome hiked his robe up yet farther, the girl gasped.

"What's that? That thing hanging between your legs."

Iktome stopped in the water. "It's a growth, like a wart. It was put there by a sorcerer." He sighed. "It's heavy, and it gets in the way, I can assure you, my young friend. And it hurts. I wish I could get rid of it."

"We could cut it off," the girl suggested.

"Oh, no, NO," Iktome said, cringing slightly. "The sorcerer . . . well, there's only one way to get rid of it. If we put it there, between your legs. . . ."

The girl thought this a strange, even unattractive idea, but she decided that women should help one another and agreed. So they crossed to the other bank and lay down on the soft grass. Soon enough, Iktome rolled over on top of the girl and entered her.

"Ooh!" she said. "That hurts."

"It hurts me even more," panted Iktome, and soon he was finished and rolled off.

"Look," the girl said, smiling happily. "It's working. It's gotten smaller."

"We'll do it again, and maybe it will disappear altogether." And Iktome mounted her again.

"It's grown again," she said. "But it doesn't hurt me so much. Does it hurt you still?"

Iktome labored away, and when he finished he said, "Yes, little sister, the pain is very great. But I am brave. I can take it."

Twice more Iktome labored and afterward the girl said, "I don't know, older sister. It is still there. We don't seem to be making much progress. You may never get rid of that thing."

"Perhaps. But we should keep trying. Do you agree?"

And the girl, who had forgotten by now why she had set out across the river, agreed.

(Leeming and Page, *God* 50–51; Erdoes and Ortiz 358–59
from Pine Ridge Indians)

The dominant trickster of the Northwest is Raven. Early in this century William Tate, a Tsimshian Indian of British Columbia, told a series of Raven tales that form a Raven Cycle—in effect, a little epic. The cycle tells of trickster tricks and creative powers. It contains a miraculous conception, the theft of light and of fire, and it describes of the origins of things. The theft-of-fire motif is, of course, common in world mythology.

Tsimshian: Raven

At this time the animal people lived in a village at the tip of the Queen Charlotte Islands. It was always dark. The chief's beloved (and spoiled) son grew ill and died, and his parents wailed and moaned for days, demanding also that the others in the village join in the mourning. Then one day the mother went to the loft where the boy's body had been put and she saw a young man who shone with the brightness of fire.

The young man explained that Heaven was irritated by all the wailing and had sent him down to calm the peoples' minds and hush them up. Both parents were overjoyed, thinking that this was their son returned to them from the dead. But the young man refused to eat and the mother began to worry, fearing that he might die again if he didn't eat. She tried one food after another, but nothing would awaken the young man's appetite.

He had noticed two of his father's slaves—a male and a female, both named A Mouth at Each End. These two ate large quantities of food.

"You don't want to be like us," the female slave said. "We eat our own scabs to get hungry." At this, the male slave scraped a scab from his leg and gave it to the young man in a dish of whale meat. The young man tried it, and grew hungry.

After that, he did nothing but eat, growing bigger and bigger, until the town's entire store of food was gone. By now his father the chief was ashamed, and gave him the skin of a raven to wear, and called him Giant. He handed Giant a bladder full of seeds and told him to fly over to the mainland and plant berries on the hillsides and put fish eggs in the streams so there would plenty for him to eat. He also gave him a round stone to rest on when he got tired.

On the way across the water, Giant dropped the stone, and it became a large rock which he rested on. Later he flew on, and after scattering the fish eggs and sowing the seeds, he thought it would be easier to collect food if there was light.

Now, he knew light was to be found in heaven, so he flew up through the clouds in the form of the raven, and there he found the daughter of heaven's chief about to drink from a pot of water. He changed himself into a cedar leaf and floated in the water, and the girl swallowed him and got pregnant.

So Giant was soon born into the sky chief's house and stole daylight, which he found hanging from the ceiling in a box. He took it back to earth. Where he landed, the frog people were fishing in the dark. He told them to throw him a candle fish. The frog people refused, so he opened up the box to spite them, and the world was filled with light.

People started calling him Chemsen, and as he wandered along on the earth he had many adventures and accomplished many things. He met Stone and Elderberry, who were arguing about which of them would be first to give birth. If it were to be Stone who delivered first, all the creatures would live forever. But Chemsen reached over and touched Elderberry, and she delivered first. That's why people die and why elderberries grow on their graves.

In this way, Chemsen the Raven went about stealing fire for the people, making the tides come and go, making it so that the animals and the people had to couple to make children, teaching people how to cook fish. Oh, Chemsen did plenty of things on this earth before he turned into a stone shaped like his former self. But somewhere to the east he still lives, and if you are wandering that way, he might help you.

(Bierhorst, Mythology 28–32 from Henry Tate via Boas,
"Tsimshian" 58–105)

A popular Algonquian trickster cycle in the Northeast Woodlands (especially among the Ojibway and the Menominee) is that of Manabozho (sometimes known as Michabo or Nanabush). He is perhaps related to Mastshingke the Hare of the Siouan Omaha. Manabozho most often appears as a human—sometimes as a healer with a medicine bag. As he helps the people and tries to teach them right ways, he is a culture hero as much as a trickster. His culture hero aspect is shown in his monster slayings and in the many versions of the story of his miraculous conception; his father is probably the North Wind, who lifted the skirt of a young girl who happened to face north at the wrong—or right—time. Manabozho also indulges the usual trickster appetites and, as in this story, plays a role in creation, often by being the cause of a particular creature's characteristics. Here the arch trickster takes revenge on a lesser trickster called Buzzard.

Algonquian: Manabozho and Buzzard

One time while Buzzard was soaring along, he saw Manabozho walking below him. He dropped down a bit and heard Manabozho say, "You must be real happy up there soaring through the air where you can see what is going on down here. Would you take me on your back, so I can see?"

Buzzard agreed and flew down to the ground. Manabozho walked up to him and saw that he had a slippery back. "You'll have to be careful flying so I don't slide off," Manabozho said, and Buzzard agreed, even though he had it in mind to play a trick.

Manabozho climbed on and Buzzard took off and soon they were soaring high in the air. Manabozho was a bit scared, but he hung on gamely as Buzzard tipped from side to side, making circles. Manabozho looked down at the ground, seeing what was going on, but just then Buzzard made a sharp turn and Manabozho lost his grip and slid off, falling to the ground like an arrow. He hit the ground so hard he was knocked senseless, while Buzzard circled in the sky, watching.

Manabozho lay for a long time all doubled up like he was dead, but eventually he came to and saw something nearby staring at him. He didn't know who it was, so he reached out for it with his hands and realized it was his own buttocks. He jumped up and heard Buzzard laughing from up there.

"I'll get even," Manabozho called out. "I've got more power than you."

Buzzard said, "No you won't. You can't fool me because I can watch you."

Manabozho walked on and Buzzard flew off. So Manabozho went to a place visible from great distances and from all directions and there he changed himself into a dead deer. He knew that Buzzard had decided to live on dead fish and dead animals. Soon all the bugs and other creatures that live on dead animals gathered around, and Buzzard saw the birds circling the body. He flew over and looked to see if it was Manabozho trying to fool him.

"No," he said to himself, "that's really a dead deer." So he settled down next to the body and began to pick a hole in its thigh. Deeper and deeper into the fleshy thigh he picked until his head and neck were buried each time he reached in.

Suddenly Manabozho pinched his flesh together around Buzzard's neck and head and jumped up.

"Hah! I caught you, Buzzard. See if you can escape."

57

So Buzzard tugged and tugged and finally his neck and head came out, but without any feathers—all he had there was naked red skin.

"That's your punishment, Buzzard. You'll go through the world with no feathers on your head, and you'll stink because of what you eat."

(Thompson, *Tales* 57–59 from Hoffman)

A trickster–culture hero almost human in form is Glooscap among the East Coast Algonquian tribes (Maliseet, Penobscot, and others). In this fablelike myth the tricks of the trickster are clearly meant to teach a moral about greed.

Algonquian: Glooscap Grants Three Wishes

It was said that Glooscap, the lord of all men and all beasts, would grant a wish to anyone who came to him, and hearing this, three men said they would try to reach him. One of these men was a Maliseet; the other two, Penobscots. It took them seven years of hard journeying, during which they suffered greatly, but finally they arrived, and Glooscap welcomed them and entertained them in his house. When it came time for them to leave, he asked them what they wanted.

The oldest of the three—who was a simple fellow without any honor or standing at home because he was not skilled at hunting—said he would like to be a skilled hunter. Glooscap gave him a flute and told him it had the power to persuade animals to follow him. So the man thanked Glooscap and left for home.

The second man answered Glooscap's question by saying he would like to enjoy the love of many women, more women indeed than he could use. At first Glooscap frowned, hearing this, but then he smiled and gave the man a bag, which he said should not be opened until the man reached home. So the second man thanked Glooscap and left.

The third man was a handsome fellow, who did little but amuse people, and when asked what he wanted, he replied that he had his heart set on gaining the power to make some funny sound—like farting or belching. He told Glooscap that the Wabanake always laughed when someone did this.

Again, Glooscap smiled and handed the man a root, telling him that eating it would confer on him the power he sought, but he cautioned him not to eat it until he got home. Happy, the man thanked Glooscap and left.

The return journey took only seven days. The hunter walked happily through the woods, his flute in his pocket, pleased to know that as long as he lived he would have plenty of venison.

The man who loved women wondered, as he walked along, if Glooscap's magic would really work. So he opened the bag and suddenly the air was filled with hundreds of beautiful black-eyed girls with flowing black hair, all swarming around him. They were wild with passion and threw their arms around him and kissed him, and he responded eagerly. Thicker and thicker they crowded around him, ever more passionate, ever wilder in their embraces.

The man realized that here he had more than he could handle. He begged for air, but the passionate girls would hear none of it. He tried to escape but couldn't. Panting, crying out for a breath, he smothered. Later he was found dead, but there was no sign of those girls.

The third man was walking along toward home, thinking about the gift Glooscap had given him. Ignoring Glooscap's warning, he pulled out the root and ate it. And he emitted a wonderful, mystical sound that rang out over the hills, echoing about the land, until an owl heard it and answered back. This, the young man thought, was wonderful indeed. So on he walked, making the noise again and again.

Before long he was getting tired and hungry. He saw a deer and drew an arrow to his bow. Just as he was about to let it loose, the strange and mystical sound erupted again. The deer bounded off and the young man cursed his luck.

By the time he reached home, he was half dead from hunger. All the game he saw had fled before his magical sound. The people in town laughed a little at his sound, and that cheered him up a bit, but as the days wore on, the people lost interest and didn't laugh anymore. They began to avoid him, and after a while his life—with its miraculous sound—grew too lonely and burdensome, so he went into the woods and killed himself.

(Erdoes and Ortiz 365–67 from Leland)

The Dying God or Goddess

The dying deity is an archetype that in much of the world has been associated with fertility. Probably established in the Neolithic period as a mythical metaphor for the agricultural process whereby the seed—the dead god—is planted in the Great Mother, earth, in order to generate the rebirth of plants, the figure takes particularly vivid form in the ancient religions of the Middle East. In Sumer and Babylon the god Dumuzi, or Tammuz, died for Inanna/Ishtar. In Egypt the great god Osiris was killed by his brother Seth and revived by his sister-wife Isis; he became the god of grain. In Greece Dionysius journeyed to the underworld and, in some versions of his myth, was dismembered and restored to life; he also was associated with crops. And in Palestine the soon-to-be-resurrected Jesus hung on the cross-tree as the new fruit of life for Christians. These gods are all scapegoat figures—beings who, like some purely human heroes, die and in some way bring boons to their people; they die for the people in order that the people may live. They become themselves the "bread of life," and often there are rituals by which the god is eaten in some way. In short, the dying god's death is a mystery in that it engenders life because of the vegetation the death brings or because of the spiritual possibilities the death signifies.

The dying-god concept exists among Native Americans, usually in connection with replenishing crops or hunted animals. For the traditional Indian, survival depends in part on a delicate balance between the needs and powers of nature's animals and plants and the needs of human beings. A deep harmony within life is established through myths of a dying god or goddess and by rituals in honor of slain animals, the planted and harvested crops, and the sun and rain needed to nourish them. Among other things this harmony requires that people demonstrate self-control and honor the spirit in all things. In some cases, under the influence particularly of the Indians of Central and South America, there may even have been North

American rituals of human sacrifice to make payment to the spirit world embodied in animals and the fruits of nature.

Maize, or Indian corn, is a crop central to the lives of many tribes; it was probably first crossbred and planted by the Olmec Indians in Mexico some eight thousand years ago, and evidence of it has been found in North America dating to 5500 B.C.E. The several dying-god/ goddess myths that exist in all likelihood serve as narrative background for agricultural ceremonies in connection with corn. These include ritual acts of sacrifice and the ubiquitous vision quest, in which a child on the verge of adulthood goes into the wilderness alone and fasts until he encounters the spirit world. The vision quest itself is a death and resurrection of sorts: through it the child is symbolically sacrificed and the adult is born. The process involves the seeking of a particular spirit helper who will guide the individual through life. The story below is an Ojibway myth of the corn spirit Mondawmin. It is a myth that speaks to the fact that corn was brought into the world not only with spirit help but by human effort.

Ojibway: How Corn Came to the People

When the youth Wunzh reached the proper age, his father built him a lodge in a remote place where he could fast and find his guardian in life. It was spring and, in the first days of his fasting, Wunzh walked in the woods each morning, musing on the first shoots of plants and flowers that were coming alive in the warming earth.

He hoped this would store in his mind pleasant thoughts for dreams each night. Often on these strolls he wondered how the plants grew—some sweet like berries, others poisonous, others full of medicine. Maybe if he knew such things, he could bring something new to his people.

As days passed, Wunzh grew too weak for such wandering, so he lay in his lodge, praying that he would dream of something that would help his people. Increasingly dizzy, he even wondered why the Great Spirit had not made things easier for his people.

61

On the third day, he saw a figure descend from the sky. It was dressed in rich yellow and green garments, with a great plume of golden feathers swaying on its head. With a dreamlike grace, it entered Wunzh's lodge and explained that it had been sent by the Great Spirit, who had found Wunzh's prayers unusual:

"You don't seem to want the glory of the warrior, but only something good for your people." The visitor went on to explain that this was possible on the condition that Wunzh wrestle with him.

Wunzh's heart sank. He was already weak from fasting. What hope did he have? But he gathered up his courage, engaged the figure, and wrestled until he was utterly exhausted and could wrestle no more. The figure stopped, smiled, and said, "That's enough for now. You did well. I'll come again to try you." And off he went, ascending into the light of the sun.

The next day, he came again, and again challenged Wunzh, who was by now even weaker. But the weaker his body, the greater, it seemed, was his courage and determination. Again they fought—long and hard—and again the visitor broke it off, promising to come once more for the final trial. Wunzh collapsed in an exhaustion near death.

The next day, after the wrestling had begun, the heavenly visitor suddenly stopped and declared himself beaten. He sat down next to the youth and told him the Great Spirit was pleased with his courage. Now he would receive the instructions he had prayed for.

"Tomorrow," the visitor said, "is the seventh day of your fast. Your father will come with some food for strength and I will come again, and you will win. Afterward, you must strip my clothes from me, put me on the ground, and take away all the weeds that grow there. Then you must bury me. Do not let weeds grow there, but come from time to time to see if I have returned. And then you will have your wish and be able to teach your people what you want them to know."

In the morning Wunzh's father came with food, and the youth said he would wait until sundown to eat it. And when the visitor came again, Wunzh seized him with strength that amazed the youth, threw him down onto the ground, and stripped off his yellow and green clothes. Seeing that the figure was dead, he buried him as he had been instructed to do, and returned to his father's lodge to eat.

In the days that followed, Wunzh would go off unannounced to the spot where he had buried his friend, and he kept the weeds away. Toward the end of the summer, he came to the spot and found a tall, graceful plant with clusters of yellow on its side, long green leaves, and a graceful plume of gold nodding from the top.

"It is my friend," Wunzh said to himself, and suddenly he knew his friend's name: Mondawmin. He ran to fetch his father and told him that this was what he had dreamed of in his fast. If the people cared for his friend the way Wunzh had been instructed, they would no longer have to rely only on the hunt or fishing the waters. With that, he showed his father how to tear off the yellow clusters, as he had torn off the garments before, and he showed how to hold the ears to the fire to turn them brown. The whole family then gathered for a feast upon this newly grown presence in their lives, and they expressed their lasting thanks to the spirit, the beautiful visitor, who had given it to them.

And so human beings guided by the spirit brought corn into this world.
(Leeming and Page, *God* 71–74; Schoolcraft, *Myth* 99–104)

The sacrificed corn spirit in Native American mythology is more often than not a female figure, generally known as Corn Mother. The New England Wabanaki Corn Mother's hair is blond, the color of corn tassels. Some Iroquoian-speakers, also from the East, say that corn grows from the breasts of the dead Corn Mother, who was the creator's mother and, thus, also Mother Earth herself. Beans and squash grow from the rest of her body. The mother dies in winter but gives life in the spring. The Arikara Indians of the plains have a myth in which corn springs from the body of the murdered Corn Mother. For some of the Keresan people of the Southwest, corn originated when Corn Mother planted her heart and announced that corn would be for the people as the milk from her breasts. The Corn Mother myths resemble myths of other parts of the world, like the stories about the African Wanjiru and the Indonesian Hainuwele, maidens who die so that crops may be born. In the Penobscot myth it is First Mother who becomes Corn Mother.

Penobscot: First Mother, Corn Mother

One day before there were people on earth, a youth appeared, born of the sea and wind and sun. Coming ashore, he joined the All Maker and, together, when the sun was at the zenith and especially warm, they set about creating all sorts of things. At this point a drop of dew fell on a leaf and, warmed by the sun, became a beautiful young maiden, who proclaimed, "I am love, giver of strength. I will provide for people and animals and they will all love me."

The All Maker was delighted, as was the youth, who married this extraordinary girl. They made love and she conceived, becoming the First Mother as their children, the people, were born. The All Maker handed down instructions about how the people should live. With his tasks complete, he retired to a place far in the north.

The people became expert hunters and they multiplied, eventually reaching such numbers that the game began to run out. Starvation stalked them, and their First Mother grew sad. She grew even sadder when her children came to her and asked her to feed them. She had nothing to give them, and she wept.

Seeing her cry, her husband was alarmed and asked what he could do to make her happy. First Mother said that there was only one thing he could do to stop her from weeping. "You must kill me," she said. Her husband was thunderstruck and refused. Instead, he sought out All Maker in the north and asked his advice.

The wise old All Maker said the man had to do what his wife asked, and the husband returned home, now weeping himself. And First Mother told him that when the sun was at its highest in the sky, he should kill her and have two of her sons drag her body over the empty parts of the earth, pulling her back and forth by her silky hair until all her flesh had been scraped from her body. Then they were to leave, waiting until seven moons had come and gone before returning. At that time they would find her flesh, lovingly given, and it would feed the people and make them strong for all time.

So these sad instructions were carried out, and after seven moons had come and gone, her children and their children returned. They found the earth covered with green plants with silken tassels, and the fruit—their mother's flesh—was sweet and tender. As instructed, they saved some of it to be planted in the earth at a later time. In this way First Mother's flesh and her spirit are renewed every seven moons and sustain the flesh and the spirit of her children.

In the clearing where they had buried her bones, the people found another plant, a fragrant one that was their mother's breath. Her spirit told them that these were sacred leaves, that they should burn them to clear their minds and lift their hearts, and make their prayer effective.

And so the people remember their mother when they smoke and when they eat corn, and in this way she lives, her love renewing itself over and over again from generation to generation.

(Leeming and Page, *Goddess* 75–77; Erdoes and Ortiz 12–13 from Nicolar)

The Cherokee myth of the hunter Kanati and his wife, Selu (Corn), is typical of another approach to the Corn Mother story, in which the people are at first disgusted by the realities of what is a metaphor for the agricultural process.

Cherokee: Selu, Corn Mother

Each time that Kanati, the lucky hunter, went into the woods, he returned with a fine load of game for his wife, Selu, whose name means corn, and their little boy. Selu would wash the meat by the riverside, and in time some of the blood rose up and formed another little boy, whom they called He Who Grew Up Wild.

The two boys got curious about how Kanati always brought home such fat bucks, does, and turkeys. So one day, unbeknown to him, they followed

65

him. In the far western mountains they saw him pull a big slab of rock back from the mouth of a cave, and out came a deer, which Kanati shot with an arrow.

A few days later, the two boys snuck off to the cave by themselves and heaved the rock slab back. Out came a deer, but they weren't quick enough to shoot it. In their confusion, they didn't push the slab back soon enough either, so all the birds and animals escaped. To this day, the animals have been scattered all through the forest, and hunting is much more difficult.

The boys were hungry, and they had no meat. They spied on their mother, watching her produce corn and beans. This she did by rubbing her stomach and armpits. The boys were disgusted, watching this, and refused to eat the food when she offered it to them. They were afraid that she was a witch, and they planned to kill her.

Knowing what was in their minds, their mother agreed, telling them to kill her and bury her body and then keep watch over it that night. This they did, and the next morning corn had grown up where she was buried, ready now for harvest.

People from far and wide heard about this, and they came asking for corn. The boys gave them some, but cautioned them to keep watch each night of the seven days it would take them to journey home. On the seventh night, though they tried to stay awake, the people fell asleep. For that reason corn doesn't grow so rapidly any more, and farming is hard work.

(Bierhorst, *Mythology* 188–90 from Mooney, *Cherokee*)

Another Native American, if non-Indian, myth of the dying goddess is that of Sedna, who is sacred to the Inuit of the northlands. While it could be argued that Sedna does not die, the fruits of nature come from her dismembered body parts and she reigns from the bottom of the sea as the supreme deity of the Inuit people (see the Oqomuit Sedna myth in part one, above).

An important version of the dying-god archetype exists in the Animal Master figure who dies ritually so that the hunt may succeed. In a sense, the Animal Master is a shaman and a trickster as he can transcend the usual boundaries of existence. The most popular of the Animal Masters is a great bear. There are Bear Man and Mother Bear myths in most regions of North America. In this Cherokee myth we find the Animal Master and what is, in effect, the training of a bear shaman through an act of sacrifice.

Cherokee: The Magic Bear

A man trekked into the mountains bent on killing a bear. Eventually he spotted one and shot it with an arrow. The bear spun around and ran noisily into the sun-dappled forest, crashing through the underbrush. The hunter pursued, shooting arrow after arrow at the bear, but the wounded bear simply would not fall.

Finally, the bear stopped and pulled the hunter's arrows from its body and held them out.

"There's no use shooting these arrows at me," the bear said. "You can't kill me." The hunter realized that this was a medicine bear, protected by magic. "Come to my house," the bear said. "We can live together."

The hunter feared for his life, but the bear knew his thoughts. "No, no," it said. "I won't hurt you." Then the hunter wondered what he would eat if he lived with this magical bear. And the bear said, "There will be plenty to eat."

So the hunter followed along until they came to a hole in the side of the mountain. "This isn't where I live," the bear explained, "but there's going to be a council here, and we should attend it to see what they do."

Inside, the hole widened out into a vast cave with houses ringing its sides. Many bears had assembled there already—old bears and young, bears of all colors—and the chief was a huge white one. The hunter and his companion slipped into a corner to wait for the council to begin, but the bears began to sniff the air and complain about the bad smell. Hearing this, the bear chief said, "Don't make rude comments. It is only a stranger who has joined us. Leave him alone."

The council meeting concerned the growing scarcity of food in the mountains, but some bears had found a new feeding ground where chestnuts and acorns were plentiful, so the bears held a dance of celebration and thanks. Later the bears filed out of the big cave and went home. The hunter and his companion left as well, and eventually they came to another hole, the bear's home, and went inside.

Knowing the hunter was hungry, the bear rubbed his stomach, and his paws filled up with huckleberries, blackberries, and acorns—enough for both of them to live through the cold sleep of winter when time stands still. As the winter wore on, the man grew long hair on his body, like that of the bear, and he learned the ways of bears.

Spring came and the earth began to warm, and the bear said, "Your people down below, they are getting ready to come into the mountains for a big hunt. They will find this cave and kill me. They will take away my clothes and cut me into pieces. No, no, they won't kill you. They'll take you home with them. Don't be afraid."

And soon, when the earth was a little warmer, the bear said, "This is the day they come. Their dogs, the split-noses, will find me, and the men will find me and drag me out and cut me up. But when they are taking me away, look back and you will see something."

Sure enough, the dogs approached and barked, the men shot arrows into the cave, killing the bear, and they dragged him out and skinned and quartered him. Then they looked back in the cave, thinking they saw another bear in there. The hunter quivered in fear, but the men realized that, under the long, bearlike fur, it was the hunter who had disappeared a year before. They invited him to come home with them.

Before leaving, according to instructions given by the bear, the bear man piled leaves over the bloody spot where his animal companion had been skinned and quartered. Sadly he set off after the men, but then he paused and turned around. And from under the leaves the bear rose up on his hind legs and shook his great shoulders. Then he dropped to the ground and disappeared into the warming forest.

(Leeming and Page, *God* 14–16; Mooney, *Cherokee* 327–29)

The dying-god motif takes on particular importance for several tribes in the southern regions of the Southwest and Far West. The Mojave Indians tell how the culture hero–god Matavilya is killed by his daughter, Frog, who gains power over him by eating his feces. The hero is then cremated after the trickster-transformer-creator, Coyote, steals his heart and, in some versions, eats it, presumably making the hero in some sense immortal and suggesting a ritual eating in connection with death. The Matavilya myth is deeply rooted in southwestern shamanism—Frog is a shaman who has become a sorcerer—and in rituals of cremation. Takic- and Yuman-speaking Indians have a similar myth, and so do the Pima, whose hero god, Elder Brother, is killed only to revive to lead a war against the rival Hohokam.

The best known of the Frog and dying-god myths is that of Wiyot, the hero of the Luiseño and Gabrielino Indians of the Los Angeles area, who brought the people to a place called Temecula. There the people were able to raise the sun above to a place where it follows a regular path each day and thus isn't so frightening as before (see the Luiseño myth in part one, above).

Luiseño: Frog and Wiyot

But all was not well. Frog hated Wiyot, the father of the people, because of the strangely shaped legs Wiyot had made for her. She spat into Wiyot's water, and after drinking the poison, Wiyot announced that he would die in the spring. During the winter before he was to die, he told the people all they needed to know to thrive on earth, and when he did die, a great oak grew up from his ashes.

Now Wiyot visits the people each night as the moon and is the center of their celebrations. The people dance for him, and cry out, "Wiyot, the father of the people, has risen!"

(Leeming and Page, *God* 68; Leeming and Leeming, *Creation* 243–44; Leach 60–63; Weigle 202–205)

Lesser Gods and Spirits

Another aspect of Native American divinity, mentioned in passing above, is the whole group of spirit figures that pervade Indian mythology. The spirit world is thought by most Indian traditionalists to exist in all things, in all aspects of life. These spirits can be channeled to good use by rituals in which priests, medicine people, religious societies, and shamans play important roles. In dance ceremonies the dancers become in some mysterious way the spirits themselves and can bring beneficial power into the tribal life. The power of the spirits can also be dangerous, especially when directed by sorcerers and witches.

Included among the best-known spirits are the Hopi kachinas, spirits of the natural world, including among their numbers the spirits of dead Hopi. They dance to bring rain and other benefits to the Hopi before retiring each year to their home in the San Francisco Peaks. The Apache *hactins*, like the Navajo *yeii*, are personifications of aspects of natural power. The Plains Indians have their less tangible spirit power, or *wakan*, which can take form in wakan men and women who have great "medicine" and in strange, sometimes bisonlike beings called *unktehi*, who taught humans the sacred dances and gave them the medicine bundle. These beings— especially the male ones—can cause floods and other disasters.

The Cree, the Ojibway, and other Algonquian Indians of the Great Lakes region have manitous, spirits that infuse everything that is, including such abstract realities as love, poverty, and childhood. The word *manitou* can refer in a singular sense to the all-encompassing power and can sometimes be the Great Manitou or Great Mystery, the Kitchi Manitou. The Kitchi Manitou, a noncorporeal reality beyond our understanding, created the world after having a vision of it. So too each individual emulates the Great Manitou by seeking the means— the "medicine," or manitou—by which he or she can most fully achieve selfhood. The Great Manitou trusts the people to continue the work of creation in their own lives. In the plural, *manitous* are individual emanations of the central manitou or of intangible realities—spiritual and even mystical realities—that come into our lives. Manitou can come to an individual in human form in a dream or a vision, as Mondawmin, the corn spirit, did in the Ojibway story told above.

The Pacific Northwest especially is surrounded by spirits who make conflicting demands on the people. One such spirit is Sisiutl, a personification of fluidity and wetness. Representing blood, tears, rain, semen, and all other fluids, Sisiutl must be treated so as to ensure balances that sustain life and prevent such disasters as floods or death through bleeding.

The traditional Native American worldview thus is essentially religious, if by *religion* we mean what the etymology of the word suggests (*religare*, to bind together). To speak of Indian gods, goddesses, and spirits as of concern only on special holy days is to mistake the whole sense of a divine reality that pervades every aspect of life, every day.

Part Two
COSMOS

A myth is to a culture what a dream is to an individual. It is a projection of the relationship between a people, their past, and their environment. A myth is a reflection of a culture's soul, its inner sense of itself.

Myths of the cosmos, or cosmic myths, belong to the science of cosmology; they are concerned with what in Greek was *kosmos*, or order. Cosmologies explain the overall order of the universe—how it came about, where people came from, where they go after death. Cosmologies deal with the big questions of nature. All cultures have cosmologies because everyone is concerned with origins and our ultimate destination. More importantly, people need cosmologies to establish their significance in the context of the outer boundaries of existence. Cultures usually use cosmic myths—especially creation myths—to place themselves at the center of the world as "the people." Naturally, each cosmology reflects the culture out of which it was born—the animals, traditions, and landscapes it knows. As a result, in creation stories cultures are given a universal context: in flood myths, for example, humans express the idea of the possibility of a cleansing sacrifice; in afterlife and end-of-the-world—apocalyptic—myths we proclaim the immortality of human consciousness in the face of the entropic decay that marks mortality.

Creation

* Creation myths are perhaps the most important myths because they place people in relation to the universe. They are cosmogonies (>Greek *kosmos*=cosmos, and *genesis*=birth), providing significance and identity by explaining where the people came from, who put them there, and why.

Like all myths, creation myths are to some extent etiological. They use symbolic and metaphorical narrative to explain what cannot be explained by existing science. In creation myths we find explanations for the origins of rituals, for the existence of sacred places and objects, and for the existence of nature and human life. We also find expressions of the relationship between humans and higher beings. Creation myths are, of course, not based on observed experience, but like all myths, they provide an understanding that is significant even in the face of modern science. A Hindu scientist might well be an adherent of the Big Bang theory of creation but at the same time have faith in the Vedic creation myth as a valid expression of a higher reality. As a projection of the way a society sees itself, a creation myth is a model. It teaches the proper relationship between humans and the cosmos, which is to say it stands for a culture's worldview and way of life, much the way certain rituals, heroes, and physical spaces do.

The complex dance of the whirling dervishes of Islam is a mystical experience of the perfectly interrelated geometric universe created by Allah and of a harmonious relationship with it. In a now rarely used form of the Christian Eucharist—a ceremony in which a sacred meal is shared—the priest ends the service by reciting the Christian creation story of the New Testament's Book of John, chapter 1 (as opposed to the older Genesis story), indicating that the service is essentially a curing rite of Christian recreation. The divine nature of the Christian culture hero, Jesus, is a reflection of the eternal "Word" ("In the beginning was the Word"), the *logos* or universal order, which is revealed in John's creation story as the beginning of all that exists. In being made new through the ritual of the Mass, the Christian is returned to the essential order that began as the "Word." The ethics of Judaism derive logically from the "just" and paternalistic creation described in the Bible's Book of Genesis. Among the followers of animistic religions—including many Native Americans—the arrangement of dwellings and meeting places is determined by the group's sense of how the world was created in relation to the four directions and to how the creator sun god travels across the sky. The physical arrangements of earthly space should signify a good relationship with the cosmic purpose.

While it is true that the creation myth reveals the attitudes and priorities of a culture, it is also true that a comparative approach to creation myths in general exposes a universal archetypal pattern—a shadow myth or collective dream of what can be called the world culture. This is a dream of orderly differentiation (cosmos) as opposed to the original and continually threatening disorder (chaos) out of which creation first arose.

The basic creation myth—the story of how chaos becomes cosmos, no-thing becomes some-thing—is, in a sense, the only story we have to tell. It is contained and represented by our storytelling, our painting, our architecture, our singing, our dancing, our love-making, and even our eating. All of these activities are forms of recreation and renewal, and we remember that recreation has as its goal what its true meaning suggests: re-creation or re-new-al. The archetype of creation lies behind our attempts to "make something" of our lives and of the material around us in spite of a seemingly relentless force that drives us toward meaninglessness or mere routine. It can reasonably be suggested that the struggle between differentiation (information) and nothingness (entropy) is the story of everything that exists.

Creation myths convey the great struggle through basic symbolic structures. Creation can be from a primal egg, or maternal mound; from the void (*ex nihilo*); from world parents who are separated—

75

usually by force; from a process of earth diving by which earth is brought up from the primordial maternal depths; or through several stages of emergence from lower worlds. These symbolic structures also can be combined in myth.

A myth that often serves as a corollary to the creation myth is that of the great flood—a myth that suggests a mistake on the part of the creator and a need for rebirth out the new maternal waters of the deluge. The flood is a kind of cosmic baptism by which we die to the old and are reborn—re-created—to the new.

Several archetypal characters appear consistently in creation myths. The creator (or, in a few cases, the creatrix, or the two in conjunction) is the primal ordered being who, by his breath, words, or craftsmanlike abilities (*deus faber*), brings cosmos out of the chaos that is sometimes clay, sometimes the fluid, or even the solid wastes, of his own body. The creator can be aided by a trickster who is concerned—often as a culture hero—with transforming and with the details of survival in the world. Frequently the creator-trickster introduces both evil and, as it turns out, the necessary element of death. The first man and first woman—our parents—are important elements in the myth, as is the flood hero, the embodiment of our constant thirst for a new beginning, for a renewed differentiation in the face of chaos.

These archetypal themes and motifs are all elements of the symbolic dream language by which the human species makes creation conscious of itself. Most of the themes and motifs exist in the mythologies of Native North America. Creation myths can be said to be the most developed of American Indian myths, emerging as they do into what is in effect a series of aboriginal epic poems such as the Navajo Blessingway or the now discredited Lenape (Delaware) Walam Olum (Red Book) (see Ostreicher). For traditionally minded Native Americans creation is a present reality, since the powers that brought it about still live in every aspect of nature, down to the smallest blade of grass. In traditional Indian life there is not the separation between mythic time and "real time" that characterizes the life of most non-Indian Americans.

Two basic forms and several related subthemes stand out when we consider Indian creation myths. These are the earth-diver creation with its diving animal tricksters and, often, its woman falling out of the sky; and the emergence myth, with the emphasis on worlds on top of one another, twin heroes, and the four directions. Each of these two basic forms is concerned, like all epic poems, with the values of a particular culture, and each explains how the given culture came to be. Underlying nearly all Native American creation stories is the belief that the people have an intimate connection with everything around them, from trees, to crops, to animals. In many stories the people at one time were animals or were able to move freely between animal and human form.

The Earth-Diver Creation

The earth-diver creation exists among the Inuit and the Athabascans of the Arctic and the Far North, among California tribes, and among several peoples of the Great Plains and the Northeast. It is easily the most prevalent type of Native American creation story. Typically, the supreme being or his assistant sends an animal into the primal waters to find mud or clay with which to make the earth, sometimes formed on the turtle's back. There are many common variations, some including the participation of a trickster in the process. Often a female being falls or is pushed from the sky and aids in the creative process on the new earth. The waters might well be seen as the unformed female principle and the diver as the creator god's emissary seed to that principle. In the ancient *Rig Veda* of India the creator god Prajapati is called the "fiery seed" in the cosmic waters. In myths around the world, the result of this cosmic intercourse is creation itself. The emissary in the myth takes the place of the creator's word, his thought, or his breath in ex nihilo creation myths. In some of its versions the earth-diver myth depicts a parthenogenic creation from the maternal waters. Whatever the meaning of it, the earth-diving act suggests that the essence of the beginnings, whether in reference to psychology or cosmogony, is in the very depths. The earth-diver has close relatives in the mythological descent to the underworld and the psychological descent to the unconscious, or "return to the womb."

Among the earth-diver myths in other areas parts of the world besides Native America is a common version in Central Asia that tells how the creator, Otshirvani, and his helper, Chagan Shukuty, noticed a frog diving in the primordial waters. After having Chagan Shukuty turn the frog over, the creator sat on its stomach and sent his assistant to dive in search of whatever was at the bottom of the waters. After a few attempts Chagan Shukuty brought back earth and sprinkled it on the frog's stomach. While the two gods were sleeping, the devil tried to run off with them and their frog-earth, but as he ran, the ground grew under them, and so the earth was made. The Altaic people of Mongolia and the Buriat and Samoyed people of Siberia tell similar stories, also including a devil figure, whom many would call a trickster, in creation. The motif also exists among the Balto-Finnic peoples of northern Europe, and elements of it are recounted in Egypt, Babylonia, and India.

The Siouan-speaking Mandan Indians of North Dakota, who are said to have migrated from the east to what is now North Dakota before they were all but exterminated by the diseases later brought by white missionaries, had elaborate myths and rituals centered around their earth-diver creation myth. Their myth is dominated by the supreme being's companion, a celibate holy figure, called Lone Man, whom some scholars see as influenced by the Christ of the missionaries. This claim is somewhat supported by the emphasis at the end of the myth on the tree, so central to Mandan ceremony, and on the relation of the tree to the "body" of Lone Man. This version of the myth was told by a elderly Mandan woman in the 1920s.

Mandan: First Creator and Lone Man

In the beginning the surface of the earth was all water and there was darkness. The First Creator and Lone Man were walking on the top of the waters and as they were walking along they happened to see a small object which seemed to have life and upon investigation they found it to be a small bird of the duck family—the kind that is very fond of diving.—"Well!" they said, "Let us ask this creature where it gets its subsistence. We don't see any kind of food on the waters and she must have something to keep her alive." So they asked her and she told them that she got her food in the bed of the waters. They asked her to show them a sample of the food. She told them she would be very glad to do so and at once she dived down to the bed of the waters and up she came with a small ball of sand. Upon seeing the sand they said, "Well! if this keeps the bird alive it must be good for other creatures also. Let us create land out of this substance, and living creatures, and let us make the land productive that it may bear fruit for the subsistence of the creatures that we shall create. Let us choose therefore the directions where each shall begin." So Lone Man chose the northern part and the First Creator the southern, and they left a space between in the water which is the Missouri river. Then, after agreeing to compare results, they began the creation.

The First Creator made broad valleys, hills, coulees with timber, mountain streams, springs, and, as creatures, the buffalo elk, black-tailed and white-tailed antelope, mountain sheep and all other creatures useful to mankind for food and clothing. He made the valleys and coulees as shelter for the animals as well as for mankind. He set lakes far apart. Lone Man created for the most part level country with lakes and small streams and rivers far apart. The animals he made lived some of them in the water, like beaver, otter, and muskrat. Others were the cattle of many colors with long horns and long tails, moose, and other animals .

After all this was ended they met as agreed upon to compare their creations. First they inspected what Lone Man had created and then they went on to what First Creator had made, then they began to compare results. First Creator said, "The things you have created do not meet with my approval. The land is too level and affords no protection to man. Look at the land I have created. It contains all kinds of game, it has buttes and mountains by which man can mark his direction. Your land is so level that a man will easily lose his way for there are no high hills as signs to direct him. Look at the waters I have created,—the rivers, brooks, springs with running water always pure and refreshing for man and beast. In summer the springs are always cool, in winter they are always warm. The lakes you have made have most of them no outlet and hence become impure. The things I have made are far more useful to man. Look at the buffalo—they are all black save here and there a white one so rare as to be highly prized. In winter their hair grows long and shaggy to combat the cold; in warm weather they shed their hair in order to endure the heat more comfortably. But look at the cattle you have created with long horns and tail, of all colors, and with hair so short and smooth that they cannot stand the cold!" Lone Man said, "These things I have created I thought were the very things most useful to man. I cannot very well change them now that they are once created. So let us make man use first the things that you have made until the supply is exhausted and then the generations to come shall utilize those things which I have created." So it was agreed between them and both blessed their creation and the two parted.

In the course of time Lone Man looked upon the creation and saw mankind multiplying and was pleased, but he also saw evil spirits that harmed mankind and he wanted to live among the men that he had created and be as one of them. He looked about among all nations and peoples to find a virgin to be his mother and discovered a very humble family consisting of a father, mother and daughter. This virgin he chose to be his mother. So one morning when the young woman was roasting corn and eating it he thought this would be the proper time to enter into the young woman. So he changed himself into corn and the young woman ate it and conceived the seed. In the course of time the parents noticed that she was with child and they questioned her, saying, "How is it, daughter, that you are with child when you have not known man? Have you concealed any thing from us?" She answered, "As you say, I have known no man. All I know is that at the time when I ate roast corn I thought that I had conceived something, then I did not think of the matter again until I knew I was with child." So the parents knew that this must be a marvel since the child was not conceived through any man, and they questioned her no more.

In course of time the child was born and he grew up like other children, but he showed unusual traits of purity and as he grew to manhood he despised all evil and never even married. Everything he did was to promote goodness. If a quarrel arose among the people he would pacify them with kind words. He loved the children and they followed him around wherever he went. Every morning he purified himself with incense, which fact goes to show that he was pure.

The people of the place where he was born were at that time Mandans They were in the habit of going to an island in the ocean off the mouth of a river to gather *ma-ta-ba-ho*. For the journey they used a boat by the name of *I-di-he* (which means Self Going); all they had to do was to strike it on one side and tell it to go and it went. This boat carried twelve persons and no more; if more went in the boat it brought ill luck. On the way to the island they were accustomed to meet dangerous obstacles.

One day there was a party setting out for the island to get some *ma-ta-ba-ho* and everyone came to the shore to see them off and wish them good luck. The twelve men got into the boat and were about to strike the boat on the side for the start when Lone Man stepped into the boat, saying that he wanted to go too. The men in the boat as well as the people on the shore objected that he would bring ill luck, but he persisted in accompanying them and finally, seeing that they could not get rid of him, they proceeded on the journey.

Now on the way down the river, evil spirits that lived in the water came out to do them harm, but every time they came to the surface Lone Man would rebuke them and tell them to go back and never show themselves again. As they neared the mouth of the river, at one place the willows along the bank changed into young men who were really evil spirits and challenged the men in the boat to come ashore and wrestle with them. Lone Man accepted the challenge. Everyone with whom he wrestled he threw and killed until the wrestlers, seeing that they were beaten, took to their heels. Then he rebuked the willows, saying that he had made them all and they should not turn themselves into evil spirits any more. When they reached the ocean they were confronted by a great whirlpool, into which the men in the boat began to cast trinkets as a sacrifice in order to pacify it, but every time they threw in a trinket Lone Man would pick it up saying that he wanted it for himself. Meanwhile, in spite of all they could do, the whirlpool sucked them in closer. Then the men began to murmur against Lone Man and complain that he brought them ill luck and lament that they were to be sucked in by the whirlpool. Then Lone Man rebuked the whirlpool saying, "Do you not know that I am he who created you? Now I command you to be still." And immediately the waters became smooth. So they kept on the journey until they came to a part of the ocean where the waves were rough. Here the men again began to offer sacrifices to pacify the waves, but in spite of their prayers and offerings the waves grew ever more violent. And this time Lone Man was picking up the offerings and the men were trying to persuade him not to do so, but he kept right on,—never stopped! By this time the boat was rocking pretty badly with the waves and the men began to murmur again and say that Lone Man was causing their death. Then he rebuked the waves, saying, "Peace, be still," and all at once the sea was still and calm and continued so for the rest of the trip.

Upon the island there were inhabitants under a chief named Ma-na-ge (perhaps water of some kind). On their arrival, the chief told the inhabitants of his village to prepare a big feast for the visitors at which he would order the visitors to eat all the food set before them and thus kill them. Lone Man foresaw that this would happen and on his way he plucked a bulrush and inserted it by way of his throat through his system. So when the feast was prepared and all were seated in a row with the food placed before them, he told the men each to eat a little from the dish as it passed from one man to the next until it reach Lone Man, when he would empty the whole contents of the dish into the bulrush, by which means it passed to the fourth strata of the earth. When all the food was gone, Lone Man looked about as if for more and said, "Well! I always heard that these people were very generous in feeding visitors. If this is all you have to offer I should hardly consider it a feast." All the people looked at the thirteen men and when they saw no signs of sickness they regarded them as mysterious.

Next Ma-na-ge asked the visitors if they wanted to smoke. Lone Man said "Certainly! for we have heard what good tobacco you have." This pleased Ma-na-ge, for he thought he would surely kill the men by the effects of the tobacco. So he called for his pipe, which was as big as a pot. He filled the pipe and lighted it and handed it over to the men. Each took a few puffs until it came to Lone Man, who, instead of puffing out the smoke, drew it all down the bulrush to the fourth strata of the earth. So in no time the whole contents of the pipe was smoked. Then he said he had always heard that Ma-na-ge was accustomed to kill his visitors by smoking with them but if this was the pipe he used it was not even large enough to satisfy him. From that time on Ma-na-ge watched him pretty closely.

(You may put in about the women if you want to).

Now Lone Man was in disguise. The chief then asked his visitors for their bags to fill with the ma-ta-ba-ho, as much as each man had strength to carry, and each produced his bag. Lone Man's was a small bag made of two buffalo hides sewed together, but they had to keep putting in to fill it. The chief watched them pretty closely by this time and thought, "If he gets away with that load he must be Lone Man!" So when the bag was filled, Lone Man took the bag by the left hand, slung it over his right shoulder and began to walk away. Then Ma-na-ge said, "Lone Man, do you think that we don't know you?" Said Lone Man as he walked away, "Perhaps you think that I am Lone Man!" Ma-na-ge said, "We shall come over to visit you on the fourth night after you reach home." By this he meant, in the fourth year.

When they reached home, Lone Man instructed his people how to perform ceremonies as to himself and appointed the men who were to perform them. He told them to clear a round space in the center of the village and to build a round barricade about it and to take four young cottonwood trees as a hoop. In the center of the barricade they were to set up a cedar and paint it with red earth and burn incense and offer sacrifices to the cedar. Lone Man said, "This cedar is my body which I leave with you as a protection from all harm, and this barricade will be a protection from the destruction of the water. For as Ma-na-ge said, they are coming to visit you. This shall be the sign of their coming. There will be a heavy fog for four days and four nights, then you may know that they are coming to destroy you. But it is nothing but water. When it comes, it will rise no higher than the first hoop next to the ground and when it can get no higher it will subside.

After he had instructed them in all the rites and ceremonies they should perform he said, "Now I am going to leave you—I am going to the south—to other peoples—and shall come back again. But always remember that I leave with you my body." And he departed to the south. And after four years Ma-na-ge made his visit in the form of water and tried in every way to destroy the inhabitants of the village, but when he failed to rise higher than the first hoop he subsided.

(Quoted from Martha Warren Beckwith in Sproul 248)

The Yokuts Indians of the San Joaquin valley southeast of San Francisco comprise several subgroups all of which have religions dominated by the earth-diver creation. Most versions of the myth include Coyote, who participates in the creation. Given the shamanistic aspect of the Yokuts religion, the presence of the trickster-transformer is not surprising.

The Truhohi Yokuts tell of a mythological time when animals controlled things.

Yokuts: Making More Land

Eagle was chief of the world, in the beginning. The only land was a mountain in the south, rising out of the waters that covered everything else. Wanting more land, the people asked Eagle for help, but it was Coyote and Magpie rather than Eagle who directed the earth-diving process. That process led to the death of the ducks who tried to find earth, but when Mud Hen dove and came up dead, he had bits of mud in his ears, nose, nails, and beak. The people made land from these bits and pieces and from chiyu seeds. When Wolf was sent by Eagle to make mountains, Coyote walked on them before they were dry and that is why the Sierra Nevada are jagged. Later, when the world was ready, many of the animals turned into humans.

(Leeming and Leeming, *Creation* 296–98;
Long 208–14 from Kroeber)

The Gashowu Yokuts say that Prairie Falcon and Raven were the primary creators, as well as that K'uik'ui (Duck) brought up the first earth. For the Wukchamni Yokuts, Eagle and Coyote are the main characters in the earth-diving myth, but Turtle was the diver. In the myths in which the diver dies in the act of creation we have an element of the dying-god motif so important in many creation myths of North America—especially in California.

This is the earth-diver myth of the Yauelmani Yokuts.

Yokuts: Eagle and the Others Make Earth

At first there was only water everywhere, but a tree grew up from the depths into the sky. On the tree was a nest, and in the nest were Eagle, who was chief, Wolf, Coyote, Panther, Prairie Falcon, and Condor. Even from high in the nest, all they could see was water all around.

Eagle thought, "We will need some land," and he began to think about how to make earth. Then he called on K'uik'ui, a little duck, and said, "Dive down under the water and bring up earth." The duck dived as deep as it could, but didn't reach bottom. It died down there.

Eagle called to another kind of duck and told it to dive down to find earth. This duck dove farther down and finally reached bottom. But just as it touched the mud down there, it too died. Then it floated up to the surface.

Eagle and the others saw a little dirt under its fingernail, so Eagle took the dirt and mixed it with some seeds he had and ground them up. Then he added water and made dough. It was in the morning that he did this.

He put the dough in the water and it swelled up and spread everywhere, going out from the middle. That evening, Eagle told his companions, "Get some of the earth." They went down from the nest and brought back some of the earth with them, and everybody waited.

When the morning star rose just at dawn, Eagle said to Wolf, "Shout." Wolf did this. He shouted and suddenly the earth disappeared and it was all water again.

Eagle said, "We will make it again." Again, they mixed some earth with Eagle's seeds, and ground them up, and put the doughy mixture into the water, and it swelled and spread out again. Again they waited, and when the morning star came out again, Eagle told the wolf to shout.

Wolf shouted three times, and the earth shook in the earthquake that Wolf caused, but it stood. Then Coyote said, "I have to shout too." He shouted and the earth shook, but only a little.

Now it was good. They came down from the tree and stood on the ground. Nearby was a lake, and Eagle said, "We will live here," and they had a house there and lived there.

(Leeming and Leeming, *Creation* 296–98;

Long 208–14 from Kroeber)

Many of the Iroquoian peoples and their neighbors in the eastern part of the continent tell earth-diver creation myths that include the motif of the Star Woman—the woman who falls or is pushed through a hole in the sky—who plays an important role in creation. The Iroquois Seneca and Onondaga have such a myth, as do their linguistic relatives, the Huron and the Cherokee.

This Seneca version of the myth contains the Star Woman and familiar figures such as Turtle and the Twins—one evil, one good—who express the typically dualistic Native American vision of the universe.

Seneca: Star Woman and the Twins

It was when water was everywhere and only ducks, loons, other water birds, Turtle, and Toad lived there. There were people, but they lived in the sky with the Great Chief. One day the chief's daughter fell sick and began to die. A wise man learned from a dream that she should be placed next to a tree and the tree should then be dug up. He told the chief about this dream and the chief did what the dream said.

But a man came along who resented that the tree had been dug up, so he kicked the girl into the hole. Suddenly she was floating down through empty space. Seeing this, the birds flew up and formed a soft net with their wings and caught the girl. When they got tired, they put her on Turtle's back, but before long he got tired too.

The birds knew the girl would need something to rest upon, so they persuaded Toad to dive down into the waters and bring back some soil. Toad put the soil on Turtle's back and it began to grow and spread out, as did Turtle's back. Soon there was earth for the girl to live on, and she was happy. She built a little house for herself and soon she gave birth to a baby girl.

Together the woman and the girl worked the land, and pretty soon the girl had twin boys. Flint and Sapling, they were called. Star Woman didn't like Flint, so she put him in a tree. She taught Sapling to make things and to hunt.

Soon Star Woman noticed that Sapling would come home from the hunt without his bow and arrows. It seems that he was giving them to his twin brother in the tree. Finally, he brought his twin, Flint, home with him, and they stayed there a long time.

One day they decided to make the earth bigger. Flint made Mosquito and some rough land. Mosquito was huge, so huge he could chop down trees. Sapling was horrified. "This is a terrible animal," he said. "He might kill the people we're going to make." So he rubbed Mosquito down to his present size.

As for Flint, he didn't like Sapling's creations—big fat animals and maple trees that dripped rich syrup. "These animals should be harder to catch," he said. So he made the animals thinner and faster, and he made the maples drip sap that had to be boiled into syrup.

The brothers' disagreements finally led to a fight, and Sapling killed Flint. But it was too late for the good brother to change the bad brother's work.

(Leeming and Leeming, *Creation* 241–42;
Leach 82–87 from Smith)

The Tsoyaha (People of the Sun), or Yuchi Indians, were originally from the Southeast, but were deported in 1838 with the

"Five Civilized Tribes"—the Cherokee, Chickasaw, Choctaw, Seminole, and Creek—to what is now Oklahoma. Their earth-diver myth, which they have passed on to the Creek Indians, contains the element of the earth-diver as trickster-thief. The sun for the Yuchi is female, indicating the matrilineal system they practiced before their deportation. It was Sun who initiated their creation, and her menstrual blood was the direct source of the Yuchi people. Unlike the great serpent in so many patriarchal mythologies, the great serpent destroyed in the early days of creation in this myth is male, and the slayer is female.

Yuchi-Creek: In the Beginning

In the beginning water was everywhere, and the question was asked, "Who will make land?"

Crawfish dove down to the bottom and found mud there. He stirred it up and took some away, but this made the mud people angry. "Who is stirring up our mud?" they demanded. But Crawfish moved so fast and stirred up so much mud that the mud people could never catch him. He kept bringing mud up from below, making more and more land.

The land needed to be dried out, so finally Buzzard soared over it, and when he flapped his wings he stirred up mountains and valleys. But it was dark in this place, so Star gave some light. It wasn't enough light, so Moon added his, but this still wasn't enough. Finally, Great Mother (the Sun) said she would make light enough for the world, and she began her daily journey across the sky. A drop of her blood fell to the earth and gave birth to the first people, the Yuchi, the children of the sun.

After a while a great serpent began to bother the Yuchi. They cut off its head, but right away it grew back. They cut it off again, and again it grew back. So this time they cut it off and put the head in a tree. The next day they found that the tree was dead and the head had grown back together with the serpent's body. They kept trying this, putting the head in different kinds of trees, but the result was always the same until they put the head in a cedar tree. Then the monster died. So the Yuchi found their big medicine.

Before long they learned about fire, and got their own language, and were happy.

(Leeming and Leeming, *Creation* 299;
Sproul 255–57 from Swanton)

Emergence Creation

The emergence creation is particularly prevalent among the southwestern Native Americans and is central to their lives. However, versions of it are told—sometimes in conjunction with an earth-diver myth—by the Choctaw Indians, originally of the Southeast, and by several Plains tribes including the Pawnee, the Lakota, the Wichita, the Caddo, the Hidatsa, the Mandan, the Arikara, and the Kiowa. Aspects of the emergence process appear in creation myths outside of North America at least insofar as these myths implicitly or explicitly compare creation to the birthing process. We find comparisons, for example, in the creation stories and rituals of the ancient Assyrians and of the Mundurucú Indians and several other Mesoamerican and South American peoples. Parallels also exist among the Bantu of Mozambique and the Papuan Keraki tribe of New Guinea.

Emergence creation typically involves the coming of a particular people into this world by way of one or more underworlds. An underworld in this context can be seen as a world womb, a place in the Earth Mother where humans, plants, and animals are conceived and gradually mature from a seedlike state in darkness until they are ready to be born through a sacred opening, such as that represented by the sipapu in the Hopi kivas. In the underworld the people undergo a process of development to prepare them for a new life under the strong light of the sun. The agricultural implications of the emergence creation are obvious, though the nonagricultural southwestern Athabascans (Navajo and Apache) have appropriated the archetype and given it exceptionally rich form. For them the myth is particularly important as a basis for most rituals, including curing ceremonies, which, by definition, mark a new beginning, and the Kinaalda, or female puberty rite, also representing a new beginning.

Sometimes the underworld people in the emergence stories are animals. The time of the underworld animal people in the emergence myth is equivalent to the myth time of other aboriginal groups who look back to a period when animals and humans lived together or were in some sense the same. In the emergence underworlds the people are usually taught by some representative of the supreme being. Usually the representative is female; male deities play limited roles in what is essentially a birthing process presided over by female midwifelike goddesses such as the Hopi Spider Woman, the Navajo Changing Woman, and the Keres Thinking Woman (see part one for other such figures). The world womb aspect of the emergence myth, the adherents of which are for the most part matrilineal (though not necessarily matriarchal) peoples, suggests an earlier time when in many cultures the earth was sacred and the goddess reigned. Emergence myths are often full epics going beyond the events of the creation and become extended tribal histories of the mythological time.

One of the oldest of the North American emergence creations is that of the Hopi Indians of northern Arizona. Both the Hopis at the village of Oraibi and the Acoma Indians farther east lay claim to the oldest continually inhabited town in North America—possibly dating as far back as the eleventh century. It seems likely that the Hopi creation story and the other emergence myths of the Southwest were influenced by those of the cliff-dwelling Anasazi, who reached their highest state of civilization in the twelfth and thirteenth centuries before disintegrating as a people. The Anasazi were in all likelihood ancestors to the present-day Pueblo groups: the Hopi, Acoma, and Laguna peoples west of the Rio Grande and east of the Grand Canyon, and the Tanoan and Keres Indians of the Rio Grande valley. The emergence myths of all of these peoples are sufficiently similar, in spite of language differences, to suggest a partial common source in the religious system indicated by Anasazi pottery and rock art.

Furthermore, the universal secrecy and conservativism associated with all but public aspects of Pueblo religions and ceremonies argue for the faithful preservation of ancient myths and, by extension, Anasazi sources, perhaps along with the remnants of the other ancient culture of the area, the Mogollon of southern New Mexico.

The Hopi emergence, like the Zuni, is ceremonially related to the initiation of boys. Hopi boys learn the myth and its significance during the rite of Wuwuchim. For the Hopi there are three worlds before this one and the Hopi are a chosen people with responsibility, partly through their complex ceremonials, for an ultimate emergence into a perfect world. The creation begins, as we saw in part one, within the mind of the supreme being, the sun god, Tawa. With the continuing intercession of Spider Grandmother, it proceeds in almost evolutionary steps through three worlds to the point where the people, knowledgeable of such things as pottery and fire but plagued by sorcerers in their midst, climb up the reed to the sipapu, the entrance high in the sky of the underworld, into the Fourth World.

It is important to point out that among the Hopi there are numerous versions of the emergence story, each of which varies from others in details both large and small. The version recounted to Frank Waters in *Book of the Hopi* is a Bear Clan version, for example, not necessarily shared by other clans. (Recall here the various versions recounted above of the creation among the Yokuts.)

Hopi: Masauwu

When the people arrived in the Fourth World, a bad thing happened almost at once. A young girl died. The chief suspected that a witch (a two-heart) might have managed to come up the reed with them and, after he questioned everyone, another girl confessed.

The people were about to hurl her back into the world below, but she said that anyone who died in this, the Fourth World, would return to the Third, the underworld. She proved this by showing them the dead girl, now back in the underworld and playing happily, so the people let the witch girl remain, realizing that she had already contaminated the Fourth World and that good and evil are always present, always at odds.

On the fourth day, they noticed a distant fire, and the next morning some of the men started out to see who might have lit the fire. They found only some gigantic human footprints. The chief decided to send four men out with a plaque on which prayer feathers were laid, to find whoever had left the footprints. Eventually they reached the fire and found a huge man hunched over the embers. They called to him three times, but he would not look up at them. On their fourth try, he said he was surprised to see them, for no one had ever come so close to him. As he spoke, he turned, and the men saw a terrible mask, behind which was an awful, bloody face.

The huge masked man accepted the feathers with pleasure and explained that he, Masauwu, was god of the Upper World and therefore their god now. Since he was also the god of the dead, Masauwu explained, anyone who died would come to him and he would see to it that the dead person made it safely back to the underworld. Ever since, Masauwu has been worshipped by the Hopi.

(Page and Page, *Hopi* 154)

The emergence of the Navajo (or Dine, "the people") is a vital feature in their rites of healing and their female puberty initiation. The most important of these rites is the Blessingway, the nine days of chanting by a *hataali*, or medicine man, who gathers most of the Navajo myths into what is, in effect, a creation epic endowed with familiar figures such as Spider Woman and the monster-slaying twins and with unusual and sometimes bizarre stories that reflect the rich Navajo imagination and the constant striving for *hozho*, or harmony with a surrounding world that pulsates with life and spiritual power. The word *hozho* is often translated as "beauty," as in the English version of the Navajo phrase "walk in beauty." But the Navajo word has both an aesthetic and a moral meaning; perhaps the closest thing in English is the manner in which a scientist uses the word *elegant* to describe a theory or experiment that is both true and lovely in its rightness.

Navajo: The Five Worlds

It begins in a small world bordered on all four sides with ocean. It is populated by insect people. While there is a difference between day (white in the east, blue in the south, yellow in the west) and night (black in the north), there is no sun or moon in the hard shell of the sky. The insect people set to arguing, mostly over their own adulterous behavior, and are ejected, crawling around the sky's shell, seeking the exit into another world.

They enter a second world, populated by various bluebird people but much like the earlier world. The exiles ask to join up with the bluebird people and are accepted. But promptly they commit adultery with some of their hosts and are, again, thrown out. Assisted by Nilch'i, the wind, they find passage to a third world inhabited chiefly by the yellow grasshopper people, and the same adulterous behavior leads to another expulsion.

By the time they arrive in the fourth word, they are much chastened and resolve among themselves to do nothing that will cause disorder. They are welcomed by a race of people who live in square houses. In this world they soon encounter Talking God and other holy people, who perform an elaborate ceremony, putting two ears of corn, one yellow and one white, under two buckskins. Nilch'i blows on the corn and they are transformed into First Man and First Woman, the true original ancestors of the Navajo. It was the wind that gave them life.

First Man and First Woman have several sets of twins and learn to hunt, farm, and make such useful things as baskets and pots. The twins marry into a group of people called the Mirage People, and First Woman, wanting to cement the bond between husband and wife, makes the penis and the clitoris. Before long Coyote happens by and blows some of his whiskers onto these organs, making them attractive (or as Coyote says, "making them shout") so that it is determined that everyone should cover themselves in the presence of others.

All went well for eight years. First Man taught the people the names of the four sacred mountains on the horizons, and taught them the ways of the holy people, who can perform magic and travel swiftly on sunbeams. But then trouble broke out.

One day, after First Man returned with a fine deer for dinner, First Woman thanked her vagina. First Man was miffed, and all the more so when First Woman explained that if it were not for the vagina, men would never do any work. They argued, and First Woman said that women did not need men, or all the tools they made. So First Man stalked out in a rage and took all the men with him to live across the river, free of women.

Both parties got along fine for a while. There was enough food to tide the women over during the winter, and the men hunted successfully for themselves. The women would occasionally come down to the river and taunt the men with lewd gestures, to make sure they still longed for the women. By the second spring the women began suffering for lack of food, and some drowned trying to cross the river.

Meanwhile sexual longing grew on both sides of the river. The women tried to satisfy themselves with stones, quills, even cacti. The men sought relief using mud or deer livers. Finally, in the fourth year of this disharmony, Owl pointed out to the men that they could not reproduce, and also that the women were in great trouble, many of them starving. So First Man sent a messenger to tell First Woman to come to the river's edge. There, she admitted that the women needed the men, and First Man apologized, and the two groups were rejoined.

In the process, two maidens were taken by a monster who lived in the river, Big Water Creature. Two people and some of the holy people tried to rescue them. They failed, but Coyote snatched them, hid them in his coat, and brought them ashore.

On the next day the Fourth World began to come to an end. A great tide of water approached from the four directions. The people asked Squirrel for help and he planted some nuts that became fast-growing trees. But they didn't grow high enough. Weasel planted seeds, but these trees didn't reach high enough either. Then two mysterious men, one old and one young, appeared with a bag of sacred soil gathered from the four mountains that marked the edge of the world. Once this was spread on the ground with the proper ceremony, a great reed grew with an opening on its eastern side. Into this the people went, and the reed grew, always above the raging waters. Eventually the people were able to climb out and into the Fifth World, where they live today. When they emerged into the Fifth World long ago, it was a very different place than it is today.

(Page and Page, *Navajo* 27–30)

For the Acoma Indians, as for most of the other Keresan-speaking Pueblos of New Mexico, there is only one underworld rather than three or four. The emergence for this matrilineal people, living in their ancient Sky City on top of a six-hundred-foot maternal mound or butte, is clearly associated with the birth process. The creation is devised from the underground mother womb by the great goddess Tsichtinako (Thinking Woman) and implemented in this world by two sisters, Iatiku (Life Bringer) and Nautsiti (Full Basket) (see part one).

The Tinde ("the People") were renamed the Apache ("enemy") by the Pueblo people they raided. They were Athabascans who arrived in the Southwest as early as 1000 C.E., but probably later. They are now divided into several groups (of which one is the Navajo), each with its own variation of the emergence creation. For the Jicarilla Apache of northeastern New Mexico the creation, even more clearly than for the Acoma, is a metaphor for birth and is particularly related to the female puberty ritual.

Jicarilla Apache: From the Underworld to the New World

In the beginning there was only water, and all the animals and plants lived in the underworld where it was dark. For those creatures that we think of as night animals, like the owl and mountain lion, the darkness was pleasant, but for the day animals it was uncomfortable. This led to arguments and, to settle them, the people agreed to play a game that would decide whether there would be dark or light. In the game, which the Apache still play today, one had to look for a button through the thin wood of a thimblelike object. The day animals were better at this game, and they were rewarded with the rising of stars and of the sun.

As the sun came to the top of the underworld, he found a hole and saw a different world out there. He told the people about this other world and they all clamored to go there. So they built four mounds—one for each direction—and planted them with fruits and flowers. The mounds began to grow upward toward the hole, but then two girls climbed up and picked the flowers and all the growth stopped—far below the hole into the other world.

So the people made a ladder out of the buffalo's horns and sent the moon and the sun up to provide light, and the four winds to blow away the water that covered everything up there. Then they sent various animals up to test the new world and finally went up themselves.

After they emerged, they traveled in each of the four directions until they reached the seas. On these journeys, the individual tribes broke off to make their homelands. Only the Jicarilla stayed behind, circling the hole through which they had come, and eventually the Great Spirit told them they could settle there in what is the center of the world.

(Leeming and Leeming, *Creation* 8–10;
Sproul 263–68 from Opler, *Jicarilla*)

The Kiowa tribe of the southwestern plains in what is now Oklahoma have a particularly unusual emergence myth with clear birthing implications. Here is the myth retold by Kiowa writer N. Scott Momaday.

Kiowa: The Setting Out

You know, everything had to begin, and this is how it was: the Kiowas came one by one into the world through a hollow log. There were many more than now, but not all of them got out. There was a woman whose body was swollen up with child, and she got stuck in the log. After that, no one could get through, and that is why the Kiowas are a small tribe in number.

They looked around and saw the world. It made them glad to see so many things. They called themselves Kwuda, "coming out."

They were going along, and some were hunting. An antelope was killed and quartered in the meadow. Well, one of the big chiefs came up and took the udders of that animal for himself, but another big chief wanted those udders also, and there was a great quarrel between them. Then, in anger, one of these chiefs gathered all of his followers and went away. They are called Azatanhop, "the udder-angry travellers off." No one knows where they went or what happened to them.

Before there were horses the Kiowas had need of dogs. That was a long time ago, when dogs could talk. There was a man who lived alone; he had been thrown away, and he made his camp here and there on the high ground. Now it was dangerous to be alone, for there were enemies all around. The man spent his arrows hunting food. He had one arrow left, and he shot a bear; but the bear was only wounded and it ran away. The man wondered what to do. Then a dog came up to him and said that many enemies were coming; they were close by and all around. The man could think of no way to save himself. But the dog said: "You know, I have puppies. They are young and weak and they have nothing to eat. If you will take care of my puppies, I will show you how to get away." The dog led the man here and there, around and around, and they came to safety.

They lived first in the mountains. They did not yet know of Tai-me, but this is what they knew: There was a man and his wife. They had a beautiful child, a little girl whom they would not allow to go out of their sight. But one day a friend of the family came and asked if she might take the child outside to play. The mother guessed that would be all right, but she told the friend to leave the child in its cradle and to place the cradle in a tree. While the child was in the tree, a redbird came among the branches. It was not like any bird that you have seen; it was very beautiful, and it did not fly away. It kept still upon a limb, close to the child. After a while the child got out of its cradle and began to climb after the redbird. And at the same time the tree began to grow taller, and the child was borne up into the sky. She was then a woman, and she found herself in a strange place. Instead of a redbird, there was a young man standing before her, and he said: "I have been watching you for a long time, and I knew that I would find a way to bring you here. I have brought you here to be my wife." The woman looked all around; she saw that he was the only living man there. She saw that he was the sun.

After that the woman grew lonely. She thought about her people, and she wondered how they were getting on. One day she had a quarrel with the sun, and the sun went away. In her anger she dug up a root of a bush which the sun had warned her never to go near. A piece of earth fell from the root, and she could see her people far below. By that time she had given birth; she had a child—a boy by the sun. She made a rope out of sinew and took the child upon her back; she climbed down the rope, but when she came to the end her people were still a long way off, and there she waited with her child on her back. It was evening; the sun came home and found his woman gone. At once he thought of the bush and went to the place where it had grown. There he saw the woman and the child, hanging by the rope halfway down to the earth. He was very angry, and he took up a ring, a gaming wheel, in his hand. He told the ring to follow the rope and strike the woman dead. Then he threw the ring and it did what he told it to do; it struck the woman and killed her, and then the sun's child was all alone.

The sun's child was big enough to walk around on the earth, and he saw a camp nearby. He made his way to it and saw that a great spider—that which is called a grandmother—lived there. The spider spoke to the sun's child, and the child was afraid. The grandmother was full of resentment; she was jealous, you see, for the child had not yet been weaned from its mother's breasts. She wondered whether the child was a boy or a girl, and therefore she made two things, a pretty ball and a bow and arrows. These things she left alone with the child all the next day. When she returned, she saw that the ball was full of arrows, and she knew then that the child was a boy and that he would be hard to raise. Time and again the grandmother tried to capture the boy, but he always ran away. Then one day she made a snare out of rope. The boy was caught up in the snare, and he cried and cried, but the grandmother sang to him and at last he fell asleep.

Go to sleep and do not cry.
Your mother is dead, and still you feed upon her breast.
Oo-oo-la-la-la-la, oo-oo.

(Quoted from Momaday 16–26)

Other Types of Creation

Several other important motifs are frequently present in Native
American creation myths. We have already seen the role of the dying
god in the creation stories of the California and southern Arizona
Indians. The Luiseño Wiyot and the Pima Elder Brother are culture
heroes–creators whose deaths are significant elements of the creation
itself.

The creation from nothing, ex nihilo, is a common beginning for
many of the creation stories, including those of the Hopi and the
Navajo, considered above, as well as many non-Indian cultures. Ex
nihilo creators create in several ways: by breath or word, as in the
case of the biblical Yahweh or the Navajo creator; and by secretions
from themselves, as in several Egyptian and other African myths and
in the following Chuckchi myth from Siberia. The Chuckchi myth,
although not American Indian, is included here because, as in so
many myths of the American Northwest, the creator is the trickster-
transformer, Raven.

Chuckchi: Raven Shits A World

Raven came into being of his own accord at the very beginning of
things, and he dwelled with his wife in a small and cramped space enclosed
in a vast gray void. It was not long before Raven's wife began to complain to
him about being bored.

"There's nothing to do, nothing to see, there's nothing. It's boring."
This went on for a long time until one day Raven's wife, having said yet
again that life was boring in this tiny space with nothing to occupy her,

99

asked Raven why he didn't make some amusement for her. "Why don't you create an earth or something?" she whined.

"I can't," Raven said, not wanting to be bothered.

"Well," his wife said with an imperious snort, "in that case, I will make something." With that, she lay down and went to sleep while Raven watched, wondering what was up.

As she slept, his wife began to lose her feathers, and at the same time grew fat, her belly swelling up until it seemed like it would burst. Even without stirring or waking up, she released two similar beings from her body—twin somethings. Like the mother now, they had no feathers. Instead, they were just little writhing lumps of skin. Raven was disgusted and said, "How awful."

The little twin somethings with no feathers heard this and woke up their mother. "What's this?" they squalled.

"It's your father."

The twins laughed and laughed, pointing at his feathers, squealing about how harsh his voice was. "How awful," they mimicked, croaking. "How awful." Then Raven's wife told them to stop fooling around, that it was rude, and they did.

After that, Raven's wife seemed satisfied. She had created what she called humans, after all, and this made Raven uneasy. He decided that he had to create something too. So he flew to the Benevolent Ones—Dawn, Sunset, Evening, and all the others who had always been out there but weren't enough to satisfy his wife's craving for amusement. He asked them to help him imagine what he should create, but they had no advice for him.

Raven shrugged and flew on until, down below him, he saw some strange-looking beings sitting around in space. He joined them and they said they were the seeds of the new people, but they couldn't fulfill their destiny without an earth. Could Raven create one?

Well, Raven had been thinking about that ever since his wife had asked him to create an earth, which he hadn't then wanted to do. But now he did, and he had an idea. He asked one of the man-seeds to come with him, and he soared up into the sky. Once aloft, he got a sublime grin on his face and began to relieve himself. He shat and he pissed and his mighty droppings fell to the ground and became the mountains, valleys, rivers, oceans, and lakes. Raven shat and pissed the world into existence.

But the man-seed clinging to him asked what people would eat, so Raven redoubled his efforts and the beginnings of plants and animals rained down on earth like heavenly hail. The man-seed asked to be put down among all these things, and before long there were many men flourishing on this new earth. But there were no women—not that the men noticed any absence.

Little Spider Woman appeared and began making women. The men were fascinated with these new things but they didn't know what to do with them. With a special twinkle in his eye, Raven said, "Let me teach you about these things."

And he taught the men about copulating.

"You see," Raven would say. "This is what you do. Now this one over here is a little bit different so you do it this way . . . and now, this one. . . ."

(Leeming and Leeming, *Creation* 53–54; Leeming and Page, *God* 139–41; Leach 198–99; Weigle 228–31)

The ex nihilo creation can also be accomplished by thought, as in this New Mexican Laguna version of the Keres myth of Tsichtinako (Ts'its'tsi'nako, Thinking Woman or Thought Woman).

Laguna: Thinking Woman

Ts'its'tsi'nako, Thought Woman,
    is sitting in her room
and whatever she thinks about
    appears.

She thought of her sisters,
Nau'ts'ity'i and I'tcts'ity'i.
and together they created the Universe
    this world
and the four worlds below.

Thought-Woman, the spider,
  named things and
  as she named them
    they appeared.

She is sitting in her room
  thinking of a story now

I'm telling you the story
  she is thinking.

(Quoted from Silko, Ceremony)

The Blackfoot people of northern Montana believe in the creator as Napi (Old Man), whose ex nihilo creation is undermined by a woman, an archetypal relative of the Hebrew Eve and the Greek Pandora.

Blackfoot: Old Man

Old Man traveled from place to place, creating mountains, valleys, deserts, plants, and animals wherever he went. He made his way north and created the Teton River. After he crossed it, he lay down to rest on his back with his arms spread out, and he placed stones all around his body. Those stones are still there. Farther north, he stumbled over a knoll and landed on his knees. To mark the place he made two great buttes called the Knees and they are still there, too. Farther north, he made the Sweet Grass Hills, the prairie, the bighorn, and the pronghorn.

Taking some clay one day, he made a woman and a child, named them people, and covered them. Later, when he took the cover away, he saw that they had changed. Several times he covered them and each time found that they had changed more. Now there were lots of people along with the first woman and her child. Old Man told them to get up and walk, and he introduced himself to them.

"I am Napi, Old Man."

Then the woman asked Old Man if the people would live forever.

"I don't know," Old Man said. "But I'll throw a buffalo chip into the river. If it floats, the people will die, but only for four days. Then they'll come back. If the chip sinks, people's lives will end." So he threw a buffalo chip into the water, and it floated, but the woman wasn't satisfied.

She said she would throw a stone in the river. "If it floats," she said, "we live forever. If it sinks, people have to die, but we'll feel sorry for each other."

Of course the stone sank, and Old Man announced that death would end all lives, and the people were indeed sorry for each other.

(Leeming and Leeming, Creation; Hamilton 25–27;
Grinnell, Blackfoot 137–44)

A motif of particular importance in several regions is that of the *deus faber*, the creator as craftsman. In this motif, a craft metaphor— carpentry or architecture, for example—is used. In the biblical Book of Job (38:4–5), Yahweh refers to his having "laid the foundation of the earth" and "determined its measurements." In many of the Spider Woman stories of the Southwest, Spider Woman's weaving talents are an important element in creation. The Mescalero Apache, who emphasize the connection between a girl's puberty and creation, build a sacred lodge in honor of a girl's first menses. This practice was followed by many other tribes, including the Iroquois, in the north, and the Lenape (Delaware) and other East Coast Algonquians. The Apache lodge is based on a universe, itself a great lodge created in *deus faber* fashion as a circle bisected along the four directions. Of the twelve poles holding up the lodge, the four main ones are the Four Grandfathers—the four directions, the four seasons. The puberty ceremony in the microcosmic universe-lodge lasts for four days and four nights and is a recreation of the principal goddess in the newly blossomed woman.

In this myth of the Yuki Indians of northern California we find a craftsman supreme being who is also, through song, an ex nihilo creator.

Yuki: Taiko-mol Makes the World

In the very beginning, foam was floating around on the surface of fog-covered waters. Then a voice came from the foam, and it was followed by Taiko-mol, who had eagle feathers on his head. Taiko-mol, the creator, stood on the moving Foam and he sang as he created. In the darkness he made a rope, and he laid it out north to south. Then he walked along the rope, coiling it as he went and leaving behind it the created earth.

He did this four times and each time the water came and overwhelmed the new land. As he walked, he wondered if there wasn't a better way. Then he made four stone posts and secured them in the ground in each of the four directions. He attached lines to these posts and stretched them out across the world, as a plan. Finally he spoke the Word, and the earth was born. Next he secured the world from the waters at the edge by lining it with whale hide. He shook the earth to see if it was secure—this was the first earthquake. And earthquakes ever since that time are Taiko-mol testing his work again.

(Leeming and Leeming, *Creation* 300; Weigle 180–81)

Creation myths, whether based on the motif of the emergence, the earth-diver, the dying god, or the trickster-transformer, whether dominated by an ex nihilo or *deus faber* creator, are the central stories, the major tribal dreams of Native Americans. Considered as a whole, these myths form a complex and revealing story of the intricate relationship between the earliest North Americans and their environment, and they form the foundation on which all other Indian myths stand.

The Flood

It often happens in creation myths that the creator becomes disappointed or even disgusted with his work. Usually it is the behavior of his human subjects that disturbs him (or her), and he can think of nothing better than to wash them away and begin again. Thus a deluge appears in many mythologies. In most cases the creator spares one man to preserve life for the new creation that will follow the flood. Usually the flood hero takes his wife and a set of animals with him to ride out the disaster in a boat made to the creator's specifications. Among some Algonquians it is the animals who save the humans.

The flood hero represents the positive seed of the original creation, which we hope lies within us all. Whether he is called Ziusudra (Sumerian), Utnapishtim (Babylonian), Noah (Hebrew), Manus (Indian), or Deucalion (Greek), he is the representative of the craving for life that makes it possible for us to face the worst adversities.

As the second stage of creation myths, the flood is one of humankind's earliest "memories." We cannot remember the events of the world creation itself because we were not yet there, but we were there, as it were, for the flood. The persistence of this "memory," expressed so universally in myth, suggests an important aspect of humanity's vision of both its own imperfections and the possibility of redemption in a new beginning. A microcosmic version of the flood is to be found in purification ceremonies such as the Christian baptism, in which the initiate "dies" to the old way in the waters of the font and is reborn in Christ. The flood is a given culture's rebirth from the chaotic but ultimately maternal waters.

The Native American flood follows the universal pattern, with certain cultural variations. Sometimes it is the creator's culture-hero assistant who instigates the world punishment. In the Zuni version the punishment is a response to incest. There are cases in which giants cause the flood. The Navajo Water Monster causes the flood when his child is hidden from him. Simple mistakes can bring about the flood, as when the Yavapai Indians of Arizona forgot to close the emergence hole. Among the Ute of western Colorado and eastern Utah, Tavwots, a version of the Great Hare, makes a deluge when his head explodes after being burned by the sun. Among the Cherokee and others, tears become the flood.

An example of a flood myth in which giants are the first creatures and the cause of the creator's displeasure is this story of the Arikara Indians of North Dakota. The myth, which features the familiar goddess Mother Corn, appears to have undergone Christian influence. The creator's assistant seems to be the same, to some extent Christlike, Lone Man whom we encounter in the mythology of the Arikaras' neighbors, the Mandans.

Arikara: Nishanu and Mother Corn

According to the sacred words, Nishanu created the first beings, and they were giants. These giants took to mocking Nishanu, their very creator, so they had to be destroyed. First Nishanu took a few of his favorites from the giants and planted them in the ground as corn kernels. Then he brought about a flood of the entire world, drowning the other giants.

Nishanu also planted corn in the sky, and when it had grown to maturity, he took an ear and made it into Mother Corn, who came down from the sky to complete Nishanu's work. With the help of Badger and Mole, who burrowed up through the ground, she led the people up and guided them westward over a great canyon, through a large forest, and around a great lake, leaving them to fend for themselves.

Instead, they took to playing games, and the games always led to fighting and killing. Seeing this, Nishanu was displeased yet again with his creation, so he sent Mother Corn back to the people, along with a man who was to be called the leader, and whose name was to be Nishanu. This Nishanu taught the people how to make war on their enemies rather than on themselves, and Mother Corn taught them all their important tribal rituals. So now the Arikara are grateful to Nishanu and to Mother Corn for all the good things they have.

(Leeming and Leeming, Creation 16; Bierhorst, Mythology 166;
Sproul 248)

Another flood myth clearly influenced by the invading Europeans is this story of the Chiricahua Apache of southwestern New Mexico.

Chiricahua Apache: White-Ringed Mountain

At one time there were many people on the earth, and they prayed to the mountain gods, to lightning and to the wind. But they did not know anything about the Great Spirit, and this made the Great Spirit angry. The waters of the ocean began to rise and soon water covered the whole earth. Except for a few that were saved, all the people of those times were drowned, leaving pottery and arrowheads around on the ground.

There was only one place the water did not cover. This was White-Ringed Mountain [just south of today's Deming, New Mexico]. Today a circle of white on the mountain shows where the water stopped, about a half mile below the peak.

When the flood was rising, the turkey ran up the mountain just ahead of the water, but the water got his tail wet, which is why his tail feathers have white tips. The people and the animals and birds on top of the mountain were saved, and from them all the creatures and people today came. White-Painted Woman and Child of the Water went up into the sky at this time.

Once the water had gone down again, a bow and arrow and a gun were placed before two men. The man who chose first chose the gun and became the white man. The other took the bow and arrow and became the Indian. If the second man had been able to choose first, he would have been the white man.

(Sproul 257–58 from Opler, Chiricahua)

The Caddo Indians of Oklahoma, like the Arikara and others, tell a flood myth in which monster-giants are eliminated. The hero of their story is a beneficent animal, the Great Turtle.

Caddo: The Four-Faced Monster and the Flood

People were terrified when the chief's wife gave birth to four little monsters, and the elders said they should be killed at once before they brought great misfortune to the entire tribe. Their mother protested. "No, no," she said. "They will turn out fine."

The little monsters grew, faster than ordinary children. They had four legs each, and four arms. Right from the beginning they bullied the other children, knocked houses over, and made awful messes, even befouling people's food.

One of the elders said, "I can see things that have not happened yet. You better kill these monsters before they kill us."

But the mother said, "No, don't. They will become fine young men, you'll see."

They never did. They killed, even ate people, and all the men in the village were helpless, they had grown so big. The monsters stood back-to-back facing in four directions, plucking up people with their long arms. They grew together into a single four-faced monster, growing as high as the sky. The only people who escaped were those who huddled right at their feet where the monsters couldn't reach because they couldn't bend over.

The man who could see the future heard a voice telling him to plant a reed in the ground. He did this and it grew fast, soon touching the sky. The voice told the man that when he saw a great cloud of birds in the air, he should take his wife and one pair each of all the good animals into the reed and climb up to the top. Soon the birds came, and the man, his wife, and the animals went into the reed, and it began to rain.

It didn't stop raining until the earth was all covered with water. Only the top of the reed and the four heads of the monster were above the water. The four heads were complaining, saying, "I'm getting tired of standing here. I'm getting weak." While the waters swirled around them, heaving them this way and that, the Great Turtle swam down and dug away the ground under their feet. They finally toppled over and drowned. Once they were dead, the waters began to go down. Mountains showed, then all the land, and winds blew and dried it. The man opened up a hole at the bottom of the reed, found that everything was dry, and told his wife and all the animals to come out.

Once out of the reed, the wife looked around and said, "Look. The ground is bare. There is nothing here. What are we going to do?"

The man told her to go to sleep, and the next morning they awoke to find herbs growing on the land. The next morning after that, they found that trees and bushes were growing. On the third morning grasses had appeared and the animals were all grazing. The next morning, the fourth, the man and woman awoke in a grass hut and saw that a stalk of corn was growing outside.

The voice told them that this would be their sacred food, and that they would have children. It also told them that if the woman planted corn and something else grew in its stead, the world would end.

(Erdoes and Ortiz 120–22 from Indian sources)

Another Plains Indian flood is that of the Cheyenne of northeastern Colorado. The Cheyenne seem to have been particularly oppressed by natural disasters caused by the Great Power, the Great Medicine Man in the Sky. The creator used the flood as a means of herding the people from place to place.

Cheyenne: Red People, White People, Hairy People

In the beginning of things, the world was a beautiful place, especially in the north, where the Great Power had created a place where it was always warm and all the animals and people spoke the same language. It was a friendly place, with plentiful food and water, and no need for things like clothes or shelter. Life was good.

There were three kinds of people then that the Great Power had made. There were hairy people, white people (who were tricky and knew lots of things, and had hair on their heads and their faces), and red people. The red people were the favorites of the Great Power. One day, after the hairy people had gone south, the Great Power told the red people to get together and go south too.

Now where they came in the south, the land was barren and food and water were not plentiful. So the Great Power taught the red people to hunt and to make clothes to cover themselves against the cold, and they had a pretty good life there. The hairy people, who were shy, lived in caves and

109

hid whenever anyone came near, and pretty soon they had disappeared altogether.

One day, the Great Power told the red people they had better band together again and go north because a great flood was coming. They did this, but when they arrived up north, they found that all of the animals spoke different languages now. Even so, it was still a good place, and the red people hunted there and had a good life.

Later they moved south again, but again a great flood came, and this one scattered all the red people around the land and they became all of the separate tribes of today. Earthquakes rent the earth, and volcanos erupted, sending flames into the sky, and the people scattered even farther. None of them was doing very well, and the Great Power felt sorry for them, so he sent them some corn to plant and filled the land with buffalo, and some of the red people established themselves in Cheyenne country and are called that today: the Cheyenne.

(Leeming and Leeming, *Creation* 47; Erdoes and Ortiz III–14 from Dorsey)

This myth of the Papago of southern Arizona concerns the leadership of Montezuma (not the Aztec king), who is the Papago flood hero and is befriended by the familiar figure of Coyote.

Papago: Montezuma and Coyote in Canoes

First, the Great Mystery made the earth. He came down to earth, dug a ball of clay, and took it up into the sky. There he dropped it into a hole and soon, out of the hole, came the Great Montezuma, leading all the Indian people behind him. Last to come out were the Apaches, who ran off in all different directions.

Now Montezuma taught the people everything they needed to know: making baskets and pots, planting corn, cooking food with fire. It never got cold and all the people and all the animals could easily talk to one another.

Then one day Montezuma's friend, Coyote, came by and told him he should build a big dugout canoe. Montezuma could make anything, but he didn't know why he needed a canoe. Coyote told him to build it anyway, so he did, and kept it on a mountain top. Coyote made himself a little boat out of a hollow log.

Before long, Montezuma found out why he needed the canoe. A great flood engulfed the land, and Montezuma and Coyote floated on its surface while everything else perished. The two friends tried to find dry land, and when they scouted out the north, they found it. The Great Mystery had already begun to make more people and animals there, and he put Montezuma in charge again, telling him to teach the people all the things they would need to know to survive.

That was all in the days before evil came and things went wrong.

(Erdoes and Ortiz 487–89 from Indian sources)

Flood myths are particularly prevalent on the West Coast. In this Wiyot (Wyot) myth from northwestern California, Above Old Man is the dissatisfied creator. The basket ark is surely influenced by the Noah story of the Christian missionaries. The creator's cleansing flood has a ritual correlative in the world-renewal cult of the Wiyot and other Indians of the area. Festival dances held at regular intervals are intended to maintain the post-flood world order. A ceremony called the Jump Dance serves to balance the human tendency to misbehave. The Deerskin Dance affirms the sacred relationship among all aspects of life.

Wiyot: Condor Floats in a Basket

The first people were born and they talked but they didn't talk right. They were all furry and Above Old Man didn't like them. It was not right. Condor knew what was going to happen. Water would come. He wove a basket, a long time weaving, and the people didn't know anything about it. The water came and Condor got in the basket with his sister. Deep in the basket, they were tossed by the waves and didn't know anything. Then one day it didn't move, nothing moved, so Condor made a hole in the basket and looked out. There was nothing out there, no people, only birds,

111

pigeons, doves. Condor got out and flew around. He found the coon's track and called his sister to him, but she didn't look right so he flew off again. Then he called her again and said she would be his wife. She laughed—she didn't like it—but then they were married and she was pregnant and people started to be born. They were really nice people, which is why Above Old Man liked them.

(Leeming and Leeming, *Creation* 287; Sproul 236–37
from Reichard, "Wyot")

The flood is but one of four destructive forces that eliminate the imperfect creations of the California Pomo Indian god, Madumda. Fire, ice, and wind follow in water's path. An important character in this myth is the creator's older brother, Kuksu, who is the center of a shamanistic cult and a secret society among several California tribes, including the Pomo, the Maidu, the Yuki, the Miwok, and the Patwin. Dances—especially the Kuksu dance itself—are intended to maintain the nurturing quality of the earth and to prevent the natural disasters so much a part of the mythology of the area.

Pomo: Last Chance

One day, Madumda decided to make the world. He wanted advice from his older brother, Kuksu, so he plucked hairs from his head and asked them to lead him where Kuksu was. He held up the hairs to each of the four directions, and it was to the south that they flew. Madumda followed them on his cloud and spent the time smoking his pipe until he got to Kuksu's house. There, as is proper, the brothers smoked the pipe four times before speaking.

Then Madumda scraped skin from his armpit, rolled it up, and gave it to Kuksu, who placed it between his toes. Kuksu took some skin from his armpit, rolled it up, and gave it to Madumda, who placed it between his toes. Each blew four times on his little ball of skin, and then the two gods mixed the two balls with some of their hair.

They stood up and faced the four directions and up and down, and they proclaimed the creation to come. Madumda took the ball and left as Kuksu sang the ancient song of creation for the first time. Madumda sang too as he flew home on his cloud with the ball strung through his earlobe. Then he slept for eight days, during which the ball grew and became the earth. Madumda woke up and threw the ball into the air. Then he smoked his pipe and threw it, burning, into the sky, where it became the sun. In the new light, he walked around the earth creating mountains, trees, valleys, rocks, lakes, seas, plants, and animals. By rolling the earth first one way, then the other, he created night and day.

Then he decided to make people. First he made some stubby little people out of rocks, then some beautiful long-haired people out of his own hair. He made bird people from feathers, and hairy deer people from his armpit hair. He made all kinds of people out of all kinds of things. Finally, he made naked people like us out of sinew, gave them some land, and taught them how to eat and to live.

In time, the people began to misbehave, killing each other and ignoring their children, so Madumda sent a great flood over the land and washed them all away. Once they were all gone, he wished for a village and it came into being. He filled the village with people from his thoughts, but soon enough they went bad, so he burned this creation down with a great fire.

He made new people from willow wands, taught them to hunt with a bow and arrow, how to make baskets, and how to eat, and then he went home to the north. But these people went bad too, so Madumda sent ice down to kill them all. He made some more willow-wand people this time, and left, soon learning in a dream that they too had gone bad. On the advice of his brother Kuksu, he sent a great wind down to blow them all away. Only the ground squirrel survived the wind, by hiding in his burrow.

This time Madumda made many groups of people from willow wands. They spoke different languages. He ordered the coyotes to watch over their villages and he taught them to grow things and to weave, and he taught them how to eat properly. He gave all the different animals their proper places, and he left, warning the people to behave. So this is our last chance.

(Leeming and Leeming, *Creation* 229–30; Leach 37–46)

Another California flood myth is that of the Salinan of the central coast. Like many stories of the mythological age, this one is dominated by animal powers.

Salinan: Eagle Remakes the World

The Old Woman of the Sea was jealous of Eagle because he was so grand and powerful. So she came toward him with her basket in which she carried the sea. She poured the sea waters from her basket until they covered all the land, rising higher and higher until only the top of Santa Lucia Peak was dry. There Eagle and the other animals gathered.

Eagle looked at Puma and said, "Let me have some of your whiskers. I have a plan." So Puma gave him some whiskers, and Eagle made a lasso. He lassoed the Old Woman's basket and pulled it toward him. The sea stopped rising and the Old Woman was so distraught that she died.

Eagle told Dove to fetch some mud, and from this he created a new world. From some elder sticks he created a woman and two men, but they were lifeless. Eagle told Prairie Falcon to take the sticks into the sweat-house, and all the animals went in and performed the ceremony of purification. Then Eagle breathed on the elder-wood people and they lived. They all made a big bower of branches and held a big feast.

(Leeming and Leeming, *Creation* 239; Sproul 236 from Mason)

These are only a few of the Native American flood myths; they exist in all areas of North America and have in common that, like the great flood stories of the Hebrews and the people of the Fertile Crescent, they are integral to the creation process, if not originally planned by the creator.

The Afterlife

The afterlife is a prominent concept in nearly every culture. The human species has difficulty conceiving of the total loss of individual self in death. The idea of the existence of some sort of conscious identity in an afterlife is more congenial. Such an existence usually requires a setting; thus, we have the many versions of the Land of the Dead, including some that are not pleasant. One of the earliest literary examples of an afterlife is the one described in Homer's *Odyssey*, which is a land of darkness, sadness, and despair, though it is not arranged on the basis of punishment and reward for past lives. Religious cultures, such as the Christian and Muslim, that stress the dualities of good and evil, tend to divide the afterlife into areas of suffering and bliss—hell and heaven. Religions that stress the illusory nature of life are more likely to conceive of the afterlife in a less physical form. For many Hindus life after death, when it is not reincarnation into another life, is ideally a total loss of individual self in the larger self of Brahman, the source of all being. The Hindu and Buddhist concepts of Nirvana do not usually involve a sense of place and are not, therefore, typically thought of as myths of afterlife, any more than is the Christian concept of the Kingdom of God. But both myths of the physical afterlife and mystical substitutes for it reflect some general human perception of continuance after death, albeit in strikingly various cultural masks.

This collective human dream can very possibly be traced to our experience of the cycles of nature and our understanding that we live within those cycles and are a part of them. The paths of the sun, the phases of the moon, the pattern of the tides, the menstrual process, and the seasons all suggest loss followed by restoration and lead naturally enough to the concept of life after death.

An important source for the afterlife might also be consciousness itself. Of all the species, it seems likely that only humans can conceive of life as a complete process including birth and death. Consciousness of the total life plot—of life's beginning, middle, and end as a continuum—could well be one of our primary defining characteristics. We are naturally philosophical as well as physical. Without that philosophical characteristic our existence or our reason for existence is called into question. That being the case, it is difficult for us to conceive of the permanent loss of consciousness. Even if we do not accept the idea of the physical restoration of ourselves in another world, we tend to have difficulty accepting the ultimate loss of the consciousness by which we perceive it. Belief in an afterlife is an almost inevitable result. In the afterlife, individual consciousness comes into its own as part of a larger collective consciousness—perhaps what philosopher Gregory Bateson meant by "immanent mind"—that informs all things and all actions. So it is that, traditionally, in the afterlife people have knowledge of the future as well as of the past and the present.

To the extent that it is possible to discuss a Native American concept of the afterlife in general terms, it can be said that there is an Indian sense of life after death based in the understanding that the human being possesses a soul that is capable of transcending the barriers of the physical world, or two souls, one for the body and one for the spirit. Some Indians believe in more than two souls. For the Mandans of North Dakota there are four souls, of which two merge to journey to the underworld after death and two remain behind—one to live in the lodge of the dead person, the other to frighten people as a ghost. The Lakota Sioux, too, have four souls. The belief in multiple souls, common also to the peoples of northeastern Asia, takes concrete form in the specific ability of shamans or medicine people to travel, like their mythological ancestors, the tricksters, between this world and the spirit world.

Through reports by shamans and the fasting or drug-induced experiences of other individuals in such rituals acts as the vision quest, Native Americans know what the other world is like. For many tribes a dead person must cross a river—like the underworld rivers of Greek mythology—before rest can be found, in a place that resembles this life, but in ideal form. Sometimes the Milky Way or the rainbow is the path to the other world. Sometimes a shaman must guide the dead there. Almost always there are particular rites that must be performed to make the process final and to prevent the negative return of the dead as ghosts. Many Iroquoian peoples practice second funerals, in which disinterred bones are reburied. Like the Parsi of India and Persia, some Indian tribes place their dead on platforms. Perhaps the most extreme North American death cult is that of the southeastern Natchez, who followed Egyptianlike practices to inter their rulers, which involved pyramid structures and riches buried with the deceased to ease the way to the Land of the Dead. Where the Land of the Dead is depends very much on the group in question. For one tribe it might be underground; for another in the sky, or in the West, where the sun goes down.

It is the Happy Hunting Ground or Spirit Camp of some of the Plains Indians that is most commonly associated with the Indian idea of the afterlife. According to this tradition, dead Indians reside after death in fine tipis in camps populated by friends and relatives. The inhabitants of the Spirit Camp spend their time hunting buffalo and singing, feasting, and dancing. Enemies used to be kept away from the Spirit Camp by being scalped after battles in the living world. Traditionally, many of the Great Plains tribes sent their dead to the Spirit Camp by dressing them well and placing them on a tree hammock of sorts. Sometimes a horse was sacrificed to accompany its owner. The path to the Hunting Ground is often by way of the Milky Way, the stars of which are the campfires of the dead. Some of the dead are returned to earth as ghosts, who often try to lure relatives to the Land of the Dead. The Lakota Sioux have ghost-keeping ceremonies in which a lock of the dead person's hair is preserved and fed for a year.

The Arapaho of southern Wyoming and northern Colorado describe the Happy Hunting Ground with great simplicity. This is Arapaho Richard Pratt's version as told to Alice Marriott and Carol Rachlin.

Arapaho: Over the Hill

When people die, they must go over a hill. There is a dividing line between the world we live in and the world of those who have gone before us. That line is the crest of a hill. In the old days, when all the country was open, and the prairies rolled as far as anyone could see, there was just the line of rocks on the crest of the hill. Nowadays, when all the country is fenced, there is a line of barbed wire there to mark the boundary.

When someone is very sick, he may start climbing the hill. It is hard work, going up, especially if his loved ones are here and calling him back. But if he is very sick and is suffering a great deal he will go on, toiling to reach the top of the hill in spite of those who are calling him to bring him back.

If he reaches the top of the hill, he can look across to the other side. The downhill slope is easy, and the grass grows thickly all the way to the bottom. At the bottom is a river, and across the river is a big Indian camp. The children are playing, splashing and swimming in the river, and riding horseback. As soon as they see the sick person, they call to him, begging him to join them. "Come down, brother—uncle—father"—whatever relative he is. But if the people on the side of the living love him enough to hold him, he will stay with them. He will know all the people in the camp, and will love them all, but the living can hold him if they beg hard enough.

This can happen more than once in a man's life. It will happen to women, too. A man who dies fighting and a woman who dies in childbirth suffer the same fate. There is no difference in the afterlife of the good and the bad; all share the same world after death. It is the Arapaho way not to judge people. This happened to me twice, on Saipan in World War II, and again in Korea.

(Quoted from Richard Pratt in Marriott and Rachlin, *American* 230–31)

The importance of ghosts in the Plains afterlife is indicated in this comic legend of the Brule Sioux, as told by Lame Deer.

Sioux: The Man Who Was Afraid of Nothing

Now, there were four ghosts sitting together, talking, smoking ghost smoke, having a good time, as far as it's possible for ghosts to have a good time. One of them said "I've heard of a young man nothing can scare. He's not afraid of us, so they say."

The second ghost said: "I bet I could scare him."

The third ghost said: "We must try to make him shiver and run and hide."

The fourth ghost said: "Let's bet; let's make a wager. Whoever can scare him the most, wins." And they agreed to bet their ghost horses.

So this young man who was never afraid came walking along one night. The moon was shining. Suddenly in his path the first ghost materialized, taking the form of a skeleton. "Hou, friend," said the ghost, clicking his teeth together, making a sound like a water drum.

"Hou, cousin," said the young man, "you're in my way. Get off the road and let me pass."

"Not until we have played the hoop-and-stick game. If you lose, I'll make you into a skeleton like me."

The young man laughed. He bent the skeleton into a big hoop, tying it with some grass. He took one of the skeleton's leg bones for his game stick and rolled the skeleton along, scoring again and again with the leg bone. "Well, I guess I won this game," said the young man. "How about some shinny ball?"

The young man took the skeleton's skull and used the leg bone to drive it ahead of him like a ball.

"Ouch!" said the skull. "You're hurting me; you're giving me a headache."

"Well, you asked for it. Who proposed this game, you or me? You're a silly fellow." The young man kicked the skull aside and walked on.

Further on he met the second ghost also in the form of a skeleton, who jumped at him and grabbed him with bony hands. "Let's dance, friend, the skeleton said.

"A very good idea cousin ghost," said the young man. "What shall we use for a drum and drumstick? I know!" Taking the ghost's thigh-bone and skull, the young man danced and sang, beating on the skull with the bone.

"Stop, stop!" cried the skull. "This is no way to dance. You're hurting me; you're giving me a headache."

"You're lying, ghost," said the young man. "Ghosts can't feel pain."

"I don't know about other ghosts," said the skull, "but me, I'm hurting."

"For a ghost you're awfully sensitive," said the young man "Really, I'm disappointed. There we were, having a good time, and you spoiled my fun with your whining. Groan somewhere else." The young man kicked the skull aside and scattered the rest of the bones all over.

"Now see what you've done," complained the ghost, "it will take me hours to get all my bones together. You're a bad man."

"Stop your whining," said the young man. "It gives you something to do." Then he went on.

Soon he came upon the third ghost, another skeleton. "This is getting monotonous," said the young man. "Are you the same as before? Did I meet you further back?"

"No," said the ghost. "Those were my cousins. They're soft. I'm tough. Let's wrestle. If I win, I'll make you into a skeleton like me."

"My friend," said the young man, "I don't feel like wrestling with you, I feel like sledding. There's enough snow on the hill for that. I should have buffalo ribs for it, but your rib cage will go."

The young man took the ghost's rib cage and used it as a sled. "This is fun!" he said, whizzing down the hill.

"Stop, stop," cried the ghost's skull "You're breaking my ribs!"

The young man said: "Friend, you look funny without a rib cage. You've grown so short. Here!" And he threw the ribs into a stream.

"Look what you've done! What can I do without my ribs? I need them."

"Jump in the water and dive for them," said the young man. "You look as if you need a bath. It'll do you good, and your woman will appreciate it."

"What do you mean? I am a woman!" said the ghost, insulted.

"With skeletons I can't tell, you pretty thing," he said, and walked on.

Then he came upon the chief ghost, a skeleton riding a skeleton horse. "I've come to kill you," said the skeleton.

The young man made faces at the ghost. He rolled his eyes; he showed his teeth; he gnashed them; he made weird noises. "I'm a ghost myself, a much more terrible ghost than you are," he said.

The skeleton got scared and tried to turn his ghost horse, but the young man seized it by the bridle. "A horse is just what I want," he said. "I've walked enough. Get off!" He yanked the skeleton from its mount and broke it into pieces. The skeleton was whimpering, but the young man mounted the skeleton horse and rode it into camp. Day was just breaking, and some women who were up early to get water saw him and screamed loudly. They ran away while the whole village was awakened by their shrieking. The people looked out of their tipis and became frightened when they saw him on the ghost horse As soon as the sun appeared, however, the skeleton vanished. The young man laughed.

The story of his ride on the skeleton horse was told all through the camp. Later he joined a group of men and started to brag about putting the four skeleton ghosts to flight. People shook their heads, saying, "This young man is really brave. Nothing frightens him. He is the bravest man who ever lived."

Just then a tiny spider was crawling up this young man's sleeve. When someone called his attention to it, he cried, "Eeeeech! Get this bug off me! Please, someone take it off, I can't stand spiders! Eeeeeech!" He shivered, he writhed, he carried on. A little girl laughed and took the spider off him.

(Quoted from Lame Deer in Erdoes and Ortiz 435–38)

Another ghost myth, told by the Cheyenne of Montana and Oklahoma, contains the motif of the ghost's attempt to lure the living to the Land of the Dead.

Cheyenne: Double-Face and Hide-the-Plum-Pit

The Double-Faced Ghost was enormously tall with immensely long arms and legs, and of course he saw both forward and backward. He could step easily over rivers, even hills, and he could catch game easily with his long arms. And he was profoundly unhappy; he was, after all, dead, and in the world of the dead he could find no suitable wife.

He roamed about the earth, contemplating his condition and occasionally hunting, and one day he came upon a tipi set up in the middle of a vast prairie. Double-Face ducked behind a hill and watched, noting that a family lived in the tipi—a man, his wife, and their daughter, who was very beautiful indeed. Double-Face was immediately smitten.

"I must have her for my wife," he said to himself, but even in the grip of passion, he realized that she might not want him, that her father might well think a ghost was no suitable mate for his only daughter. "I must prove to them that I would make a good husband," Double-Face thought.

That night Double-Face slipped off and went hunting, gathering up some nice fat game in his long arms. In the darkness before dawn, he brought a load of the meat to the tipi and left it there. The parents and their daughter were elated to find it there and their elation grew as, each day before dawn, Double-Face left yet more juicy meat for them.

After a while, the father said, "I will have to find out who is paying us this great kindness." But try as he might, he never did get a glimpse of the mysterious benefactor, and the supply of meat kept coming. Finally, one night the father dug a hole behind some bushes outside his tipi and climbed in. The night passed slowly and just before dawn, in the thin light of a crescent moon, he saw an enormous shape approach, a huge figure with long arms and—yes!—two faces, one forward and one looking out behind. He watched in horror as the vast figure dropped a load of meat near the tipi and vanished. Trembling with fear, the father scrambled out of the hole and ran into his tipi, shouting, "Pack up! Pack up our things, and strike the tipi! It's a terrible monster that brings that meat. We must flee."

So off they went, and when Double-Face returned to his hiding place behind the hill, he saw that the tipi was gone. He followed the family's tracks across the prairie and, taking long strides on his long legs, he soon overtook them.

"Wait, wait," he said in as friendly a tone as he could muster. "Please wait and hear me out. I mean you no harm. I have only the kindest feelings for you. Can we sit down and talk?"

Well, the family didn't see that they had much choice. Fearfully, they sat down while the monster, or ghost, or whatever it was towered over them, fidgeting.

"It was kind of you to leave us that meat," the father said. "What is it that you want in return?"

"I have fallen in love with your beautiful and worthy daughter. I want her as my wife. I assure you that I am an excellent provider. Haven't I proved that?"

The father found himself in a terrible quandary. Naturally, he didn't want his daughter married to a ghost, a dweller in the land of the dead no matter how present he might seem in this world. And even if the father wanted such a union to take place, he knew full well that his daughter would object. Why would a beautiful young woman want to marry this monstrously tall, long-armed, long-legged apparition with its alarming two faces? At the same time, the father was scared to displease the ghost.

Finally he spoke. "You are very kind, and handsome as well. And it is clear that you are the mightiest of hunters—just the sort of man a father hopes will marry his daughter. What young woman could object to a man like you? Since you have expressed your desire for my daughter, we are happy to proceed in the customary manner among my people. You know our custom, of course."

"Custom," Double-Face said. "What custom?"

"A suitor always plays a game with us—hide-the-plum-pit. If the suitor wins, he gets the girl for his bride. If he loses, he gives something valuable to the family."

"I never heard of this custom," said Double-Face, suspicious that maybe it was a trick.

"It has been our custom for a long time, ever since the world began. If we go against our customs, then misfortune will strike us all."

"Well," the ghost said, "in that case, let us play this game."

"Very wise of you," the father said and explained the rules again. "If you win, I give you my daughter. If you lose, you will keep giving us meat every morning—well, maybe every other morning."

"Agreed," said the ghost, thinking that however fast the man's hands were, he would not be able to conceal the plum pit from him. But the man, it turned out, was the best, the fastest plum-pit player in the world. The game began, the man's hands moving with lightning quickness, while the girl and her mother played on a drum and sang funny songs to distract the ghost. And he couldn't find the plum-pit. He lost. Graciously, Double-Face accepted his loss and the terms of the game. As long as the family lived, and even after the daughter married, he brought meat every other day before dawn.

(Erdoes and Ortiz 439–41 from Kroeber)

Among the greatest of the Plains mythmakers were the Blackfoot tribe of Montana, whose myths and legends were collected in English by George Bird Grinnell in the late 1880s and early 1890s. This is a ghost story with a distinct Orpheus theme, a theme of life restoration frequently found in Native American mythology. The motif takes its name from the Greek story of Orpheus, who was allowed to retrieve his beloved Eurydice from the underworld on the condition that he not look back as she followed him up the steep path to this world. Of course, in his anxiety, he did look back, and she was lost to him forever.

Blackfoot: Loses His Wife Twice

One time long ago, a man who was one of us got married and his wife had a baby, a little boy. But then she got sick. The man loved his wife deeply and refused to take another woman. Nothing helped his wife get well; the medicine men tried but it was no use. Finally she died, and in his sorrow, the man went away from the camp, taking his little boy. He carried his son on his back and went about the hills crying for his lost wife.

One day he decided that somehow he would find his wife. He took his little boy to his mother's house and told her to take care of him. Then he started out, not knowing which way to go. He headed for the Sand Hills and wandered there. On the fourth night, he dreamed he came upon a little lodge where an old woman lived.

"Why are you here?" the old woman asked, and the man told her he was looking for his wife who had died.

"I saw her," the old woman said, "when she passed this way. If you go over to that next butte, the old woman there will help you find her in the land of the ghosts that lies beyond."

The next day he awoke and set out for the next butte, and when night came, he lay down there and dreamed again. He dreamed he came to a second lodge and that another old woman there said she would help him make this journey. She warned him that it was dangerous, that he might not succeed. She gave him a medicine bundle to help him.

"You stay here," she said, "and I'll go first and try to bring some of your relations back here. If they do come, then you can go with them. But you must keep your eyes shut, and you must not be afraid, even though they will make fearful noises and try to scare you."

The old woman left, and came back later with one of the man's relations. With his eyes shut, he followed his relation to the ghosts' camp, and the ghosts shrieked and tried to scare him, but he kept on going until he came to yet another lodge. The man who owned it came out and asked him what he was doing there.

"I'm looking for my dead wife. I miss her so much I can't rest. My son mourns for her too. I have no interest in the other women I've been offered. Only my wife, the one I'm searching for."

The man, who was a ghost, of course, said, "This is a very dangerous journey you're taking. You may never go home. There's never been a living person here before. You come in my lodge, and stay here four nights, and you'll see your wife. But if you're not careful, you'll die right here and never get out."

That man, who was a chief ghost, went out and called for a feast, telling some of the ghosts that their son-in-law had come. He didn't tell them that their son-in-law was still alive. So the ghosts came, but they wouldn't go in the lodge.

"Pugh," they said. "It smells bad in there. It smells like a person."

So the ghost chief put some sweet pine logs on the fire and masked the smell, and the in-laws came in.

"Your son-in-law," the chief said, "has come because he mourns for his wife, and so does his son who is alone with no mother. This man here is very brave. Nothing here has weakened his heart. Have pity on him and give him back his wife."

The ghosts consulted among themselves, and one of them announced that they would give the young man a sacred pipe, the Worm Pipe, and he could take that and his wife home with him. They said they would follow the couple for four days and that the young man had to keep his eyes shut that whole time. His wife, they explained, would not be a person during those four days, but then when he opened his eyes after four days, she would be alive again.

The ghost chief told him that once he and his wife got home, they should tell his people to prepare a sweat lodge for them so they could clean every little bit of their bodies to remove any traces of ghostliness. The ghost chief also told him that he should never lose his temper with his wife or strike her.

So, carrying the Worm Pipe, the couple left, accompanied by the ghosts, and on the fourth day, his wife told him to open his eyes. He did, and beheld his wife, alive again, and he was overjoyed. He took her into camp and told the people to prepare a sweat for them. They cleaned themselves, and smoked sweet grass and purified their clothes, and hung the Worm Pipe over the door. Life went on as before.

But then one night the man asked his wife to do something and she was slow to do it. Angry, he picked up a brand from the fire and threatened her with it. He was just pretending that he would hit her, didn't intend to hit her, but suddenly, in an instant, she was gone, vanished forever.

(Grinnell, *Blackfoot* 127–31)

The Zuni tell the following Orpheus tale of a young man and his spirit wife.

Zuni: Red Plume

Grieving for his dead wife, a young man determined to follow her to the Land of the Dead. With prayer sticks, corn pollen, and an eagle feather colored with red earth, he waited by her grave one night and she appeared, smiling. "Don't grieve so," she said. "I've merely left one life for another."

"But I love you," the young man said. "I feel I must go with you." The spirit wife tried to persuade him not to, but since he was determined, she said he could follow her. But, she said, she would be invisible to him in the sunlight. If he tied the red eagle plume to her hair, however, he would be able to follow it.

This he did, and soon enough his spirit wife began to fade in the oncoming dawn. Soon only the red plume was visible, dancing nearby, dancing ahead of him almost within arm's reach. Throughout the day he followed it westward into the land of the evening sun, growing tired, more tired, and falling behind. "Wait, wait," he called, and the plume paused while he caught up. And so the journey continued over many days, the young man growing exhausted to the point where he believed he could not go on.

Just then the red plume came to a great chasm and floated across. He called out, "Wait, wait. I love you." He clambered over the side, hoping to descend and then ascend the other side, but soon found himself stuck on a narrow ledge, his footing giving way. Just before he fell into the abyss, a ground squirrel leapt onto the ledge and mocked the young man, asking if he thought he had wings to fly. But the squirrel also said he would help, and he produced a seed, wet it, and planted it. Immediately a shoot appeared and grew rapidly, reaching the other side of the canyon. The young man thanked the squirrel and crossed to the other side, where, to his great joy, he saw the red plume dancing in the air, waiting for him.

Again it moved off, and again he followed it, racing after it until his sides ached and he thought his heart would burst in his chest. Then the plume came to a vast, dark lake and plunged into the water, disappearing into the depths, and the young man knew that there, in the waters below, lay the Land of the Dead. He called out, "Come back, come back. I cannot go down in there. Come back." But the dark waters lay still before him. He waited through the night, but his wife, the plume—all was gone. He wept as the sun again rose.

There came a strange sound, the hoo-hooing of an owl, and soon enough an old owl appeared near him, asking why he was weeping. The young man told his story, of his wife dying, of following the red plume for such a great distance, of the chasm and the squirrel, and of the disappearance in the lake.

"Follow me," the owl said. "You will come and stay in my house in the mountains, and if you follow my instructions, you will have your wife back." Once in the owl's house, the young man found himself in the company of a crowd of owl men and owl women who welcomed him and bade him to sit down and eat. Happily the young man complied, and he watched as the old owl removed his owl clothes and became a man. He held a medicine bundle out, and the young man reached for it.

"Not so fast," the man said. "Be patient. I'll give this to you but first you must listen to my instructions. Now, this medicine will put you into a deep sleep, and when you awake you must follow the morning star to the middle anthill. Your wife will be waiting for you there, and when the sun rises she will live again. But be patient. Do not touch her or embrace her until you both have reached your home."

The young man agreed, saying that he would be patient, and soon enough he was sound asleep. The owl people then flew down into the lake and cradled the young man's wife in their wings, bringing her up to the surface. They brought her back to the old owl's house and put her down beside her sleeping husband.

As morning neared, he awoke, saw the morning star, saw that his wife's spirit was lying beside him, and rejoiced. She smiled at him and said, "Your love for me is stronger than any other love has been. Otherwise we would not be here together again."

They arose and left, taking the path that would lead them home. After the fourth day, the young wife said she was exhausted and asked if they could rest. She lay down and fell asleep. Her lover sat beside her, marveling at her beauty, marveling at her appearance again in his life, in the land of the living. Overcome, he reached out and touched her.

She startled, sat up, and burst into tears. "You loved me," she wailed, "but not enough. Not enough. You couldn't wait. I must die again." She faded before his very eyes, and vanished.

From a branch above his head, the old owl called out. "Shame," he said. "Shame." The young man's eyes went blank and he stared into the distance and his mind ran off, never to return.

This is how death came to be with us. If the young man had only waited, then death would have been conquered. It is a sad thing, but it may be a necessary thing, too. Think about it.

(Erdoes and Ortiz 447–51 from Indian sources)

The Indians of the West Coast have many myths of the afterlife. The following Orpheuslike tale is told by the Serrano of California about a great hunter whose beloved wife died one day when he was gone on a hunting trip. She was, in fact, killed by the hunter's mother, who hated her. As custom dictated, the people put her body on a platform and burned it.

Serrano: The Land of the Dead

When the hunter came home and learned what had happened, he was overcome with grief. He stood by the platform of burning all night, not moving, in the grip of an awful sadness. From the charred place, curls and wisps of smoke arose and he watched them through that night and the following day. When evening again came, the last wisp of smoke eddied up and moved away across the land. In the dark he followed it, knowing that it was his wife.

They came to the rock that dead people must pass on their journey. If they have led bad lives, the rock falls on them. Here the wisp of smoke who was his wife said, "Now we will go into the place of the dead. I'll carry you on my back so they won't notice you."

So they journeyed on, the hunter on his wife's back, until they came to the river the dead must ford. The wife kept her husband on her back and they safely crossed this dangerous place. Soon they came upon the wife's people—her relatives who had died before her. They welcomed her, but were not at all happy to see her husband, since he wasn't dead like them.

"If he stays here," they complained, "we'll have to cook special food for him because he can't survive on what us dead people eat."

But the wife pleaded for him and they let him stay. Even so, during the daytime, he couldn't see them—only at night were the dead people visible to him—and during the days it was lonely.

One time, the dead people went on a deer hunt and took him along, telling him to stand near the deer trail. Soon they were all shouting: "Deer! Deer!" Well, the hunter knew that deer were coming his way, but he couldn't see anything because it was daytime. But at the last moment, he peered again and saw two little black beetles. He knocked them over, and he heard all the dead people cheering. After that, nobody complained about him being there, and soon they began to feel sorry for him.

"It's too early for him to be a dead person," they said among themselves, "and this isn't a good place for live people. Maybe we should have his woman go home with him."

They told the couple they could go but shouldn't have anything to do with each other for three nights after they got home. The couple happily agreed and left, and once they got home, they were continent for three nights as they had been instructed. What they didn't know was that three nights for the dead means three years for the living. And when the hunter woke up on the fourth day, he was alone again.

(Erdoes and Ortiz 438–39 from Benedict, "Serrano")

The Modoc, of northern California and Oregon, tell this tale of the trickster Kumokums and his attempt to rescue his daughter from the Land of the Dead. It speaks to the connection between the trickster of the mythological age and the later shaman, who descends to the spirit world in the service of the sick and dying.

Modoc: Do Not Look Back toward the Land of the Dead

Kumokums and all the animals divided their year between a summer camp and a winter camp. In each camp, food was plentiful and life was good, and soon there were many, many babies—too many babies, indeed. Porcupine grew concerned about this and came to Kumokums to talk about it.

"There are too many people here now, too many babies being born. Some of our old people are dying, but there are still too many people. Now, we know that when the old people die they go to another land where they are happy. Why don't we let the people here in the village go to the Land of the Dead. They'll be happy there."

Kumokums thought about this and finally agreed, saying, "People should leave this earth forever once they have died. The chief over there in the Land of the Dead is a good man. The people will be happy there with him."

"Good," said Porcupine. "I am happy you see my point."

Five days later, Kumokums came home from a fishing trip and heard a great wailing in his camp. He threw down his fish and ran into his house. His daughter was lying still on the ground and all his wives were keening with grief.

"What has happened?" Kumokums demanded, and his wives told him that his daughter had gone to the Land of the Dead.

"No, no, she can't," Kumokums cried. He loved his daughter more than anyone, and he called out her name, begging her to come back. He sent his wives for the medicine man, who came and did his ceremonies, but still his daughter lay dead.

Then Porcupine came in and waddled over to Kumokums.

"You agreed, Kumokums, that this is how it should be. You yourself said that there should be death for everyone. You can't expect not to suffer from it yourself."

"But there must be a way," Kumokums said. "Some way to bring her back."

"Well, there is a way," Porcupine said. "You have to go there yourself, to the Land of the Dead, and talk to the chief. He is your friend, you said. But it's dangerous."

Kumokums said that he would go no matter how dangerous it was, and so he lay down and sent his spirit to the Land of the Dead, where everyone was a skeleton. The chief asked what he had come for.

"My daughter. I've come to take her home. I love her, and it was too soon for her to die. But where is she? I don't see her here."

"She's here," the chief said. "I've taken her to my house to be my daughter. Come out here, daughter." A narrow skeleton appeared, the skull grinning hideously, eyeholes black.

"There she is," the chief said. "Do you really want her now? She's not the beautiful girl you remember. Would you really want her in your village looking like that?"

"I do," Kumokums said, and the chief said he was very brave.

"Nobody else who has ever come here was so brave. I give her to you. Take her with you, and as you go, press her hand four times. She will return to living form when you get back to your village. But do not look back. Whatever you do, do not look back toward the Land of the Dead."

Kumokums agreed, and led his daughter away, pressing her bony fingers four times and feeling flesh grow there. He was elated. When he reached the edge of the land of the living, he decided they were safe. Turning, he glanced back at his daughter, but there was nothing to see but a pile of bones. Kumokums opened his eyes and found he was in his own lodge in his village. Porcupine was there, watching him.

"I told you," Porcupine said, "that it would be a dangerous journey. Now there will always be death in this world."

(Marriott, *American* 226–29 from Mary Chiloquin)

A Chinook Indian of Oregon told this shamanic and ghostly tale to Franz Boas in 1894.

Chinook: Smirking Bluejay

Bluejay's sister had been missing for a year and the story was going around that the ghosts had come and taken her away to be their bride. Bluejay asked around about where people went when they died and finally he found his way to a big town where all the houses were empty but one. Inside he found his elder sister, Io'i, who greeted him with great warmth.

"So you died too," she said.

"No, no," Bluejay said. "I didn't die. I just came to find you. But what are all these skulls and bones around here?"

"They are your in-laws," she said, and Bluejay smirked.

"Io'i lies," he said. "Io'i has always lied." But then people arose from the bones and the house was full of activity.

"Who are all these people," Bluejay asked. His sister laughed. "They aren't people, they're ghosts. They want you to go fishing with them. Go with that boy there, but keep quiet."

Bluejay noticed that all these people talked in whispers, and he couldn't hear what they were saying.

Soon they were all underway in canoes, singing as they went. Bluejay joined the singing and everyone fell silent. Behind him, where the boy had sat paddling, there was only a pile of bones. So Bluejay was quiet, and presently the boy appeared again in the stern. "Where's your fish trap?" Bluejay asked, and again there was only a pile of bones.

Finally, they reached a place on the river where the fishing could begin. Bluejay caught some branches in his net and threw them back in. Then he caught some leaves and threw them back in, but the boy gathered some of them up. Bluejay caught two more branches and thought he might take them back to Io'i to make a fire.

When they got back, Io'i laughed at him again for throwing the sticks and leaves back in the water. She took the two sticks and the leaves from the boy and roasted them. "The sticks are our trout and the leaves are our fall salmon," she explained. "This is what we eat." And Bluejay smirked and said, "Io'i lies."

The next day Bluejay went down to the beach where the canoes had been pulled up. "Look at those canoes," he said derisively. "They're really bad. Full of holes and covered with moss." Io'i got angry, and told Bluejay to be quiet. The canoes were fine, she said, for ghosts.

The next day, Bluejay went fishing again with the boy. This time he played tricks on the boy, raising his voice and turning him into a pile of bones. This time he kept all the sticks and leaves he caught, and on the way home he teased all the other ghosts in the other canoes, raising his voice and turning them to bones.

For several days he played tricks like this until everyone got tired of it and shunned him. He decided it was time to go home. His sister, Io'i, gave him five buckets of water, telling him that he would have to cross some burning prairies, but to save the water until he came to the fourth one.

Bluejay agreed, and off he went, soon coming to the first burning prairie. He poured some of his water out so that he could cross it, and did this each time he came to a burning prairie. When he reached the fourth, he poured out the last of his water but still had a long way to go through the burning grass. He beat at the flames with his bearskin, but it caught on fire and burned up, along with Bluejay himself.

That night he tried to make his way back to his sister, and fetched up on the bank of a river. From the other side Io'i came in a canoe, a canoe of great beauty, and Bluejay remarked on it.

Io'i laughed. "You said our canoes were bad—full of holes and moss-covered. Now you are dead and you see things differently."

"Io'i lies," Bluejay said. "This canoe is beautiful. The other ones were moss-covered and ugly."

They crossed over to the other bank and soon reached Io'i's house. It was full of people singing and dancing, some of them being conjurers, all of them appearing to Bluejay to be quite beautiful.

"You are dead now," Io'i said, "and things look different."

But Blue Jay didn't believe this. He cried out in a loud voice, thinking the people would fall down into bone piles, but they just laughed at him. Bluejay fell silent and went over to watch the conjurors, asking them how he could gain their powers. But they laughed at him. Each night for five nights he came and asked the conjurors how he could get their powers, and on the fifth night his sister found him standing on his head, his feet sticking up in the air and wiggling like he was dancing. This made Io'i cry, for now she knew that her brother was really dead. Twice he had died, and the conjurors had also taken away his wits.

(Erdoes and Ortiz 457–62 from Boas, Chinook)

In the Southwest, the Navajos shun death as much as possible and traditionally do not believe in a blissful afterlife. There is a vague

Navajo sense, derived in all likelihood from the Pueblo people, that the dead return to the preemergence world, which is in the north— the evil direction. Relatives meet the dead person and take him or her to the world below. A dead body must be buried immediately, preferably by a non-Navajo, and cleansing ritual precautions must be taken to prevent the deceased's return as a ghost. Ghosts of the recently departed are believed to wander about, seeking retribution for even the most minor wrongs and slights done to them in life; and indeed about half of the many Navajo healing ceremonies, or "ways," are regarded as "enemy ways," designed to cure the trouble brought about by ghosts—or witches.

The Pueblo peoples of the region generally believe that in death the spirit of the individual—sometimes the breath—returns to the place of emergence and turns into a cloud. Clouds, then, are incarnations of the dead and can be associated with kachinas, forces or spirits of nature, who in this context are beloved ancestors who bring rain to the people.

Myths of the afterlife, like those of the flood, are metaphors illustrating that life exists only in relation to periodic destruction or disintegration of formed matter. Myths of the apocalypse, the end of the world, take that destructive process into the cosmic realm.

The End of the World

Myths of the end of the world—that is, eschatological myths—are usually associated with an apocalypse, a revelation or prophetic vision. The biblical revelations to various prophets (Daniel, Isaiah, Ezekiel, and Joel) of the Day of Yahweh, the New Testament Revelation of Saint John the Divine, the Day of Judgment revealed to Zoroaster, the end of the Kali Age made known to the writers of the Hindu *purnanas*, and the Norse tradition of Ragnarok, as told to Gangleri by the High One, are all examples of apocalypses, all myths of the end of the world.

The idea of the end of the world is universal. In some cases a new world order is foreseen as a result of the catastrophic end, but the emphasis nearly always is on the end of *this* world order. The end-of-the-world archetype is, of course, closely related to the myth of the flood. Through both myths human societies express, in their own cultural terms, a sense of an inevitable cosmic intervention against human failings. The end-of-the-world concept is a large-scale expression of the human fascination with the process of death and possible renewal. Psychologically, it reflects the need to confront reality, to recognize the final battlefield, the Armageddon of the Last Judgment, where good and evil must finally face each other. In East Asian expressions of the end of the world the emphasis is not as millennial. The end of the world is seen as part of the breathing of the universe itself, something to expect and to witness rather than resist. The Native American vision seems in general, when not influenced by Christianity, to be more like the Asian than the Western concept. But many of the eschatological myths of the Indians are clearly responses to the huge and abrupt upheavals in their lives as a result of the European intrusions onto the continent, rather than what may be thought of as original or archetypal upheavals. As the Dalai Lama has said, "All prophecies are really about the past."

The prophecies of North American natives are revealed in visions to holy men or prophetic shamans, like Black Elk of the Oglalla Sioux or Wovoka, the Paiute founder of the revivalistic Ghost Dance on the Great Plains in the last quarter of the nineteenth century. The Ghost Dance involved trances in which the dancers would meet their ancestors and would wake up to sing of the joys of a renewal of the lost Indian way of life. It was based on a vision in which Wovoka was witness to the total destruction of the white world and the return of the buffalo and the old Indian people. It is particularly ironic that it was the Ghost Dance that terrified the whites and led to the massacre of 260 dancers—men, women, and children—on December 29, 1890, at Wounded Knee Creek in South Dakota, an event that effectively ended what was left of the old Plains Indian world of the Great Hunt.

The following is the historical myth of Wounded Knee as told to Richard Erdoes by Dick Fool Bull at the Rosebud Brule Sioux Reservation in the mid 1960s.

Sioux: The Ghost Dance at Wounded Knee

This is a true story; I wish it weren't. When it happened I was a small boy, only about six or seven. To tell the truth, I'm not sure how old I am. I was born before the census takers came in, so there's no record.

When I was a young boy, I liked to stick around my old uncle, because he always had stories to tell. Once he said, "There's something new coming, traveling on the wind. A new dance. A new prayer." He was talking about Wanagi-wachipi, the ghost dance. "Short Bull and Kicking Bear traveled far," my uncle told me. "They went to see a holy man of another tribe far in the south, the Piute tribe. They had heard that this holy man could bring dead people to life again, and that he cold bring the buffalo back."

My uncle said it was very important, and I must listen closely. Old Unc said;

This holy man let Short Bull and Kicking Bear look into his hat. There they saw their dead relatives walking about. The holy man told them, "I'll give you something to eat that will kill you, but don't be afraid. I'll bring you back to life again." They believed him. They ate something and died, then found themselves walking in a new, beautiful land. They spoke with their parents and grandparents, and with friends that the white soldiers had killed. Their friends were well, and this new world was like the old one, the one the white man had destroyed. It was full of game, full of antelope and buffalo. The grass was green and high, and though long-dead people from other tribes also lived in this new land, there was peace. All the Indian nations formed one tribe and could understand each other. Kicking Bear and Short Bull walked around and saw everything, and they were happy. Then the holy man of the Piutes brought them back to life again.

"You have seen it," he told them, "the new Land I'm bringing. The earth will roll up like a blanket with all that bad white man's stuff, the fences and railroads and mines and telegraph poles; and underneath will be our old-young Indian earth with all our relatives come to life again."

Then the holy man taught them a new dance, a new song, a new prayer. He gave them sacred red paint. He even made the sun die: it was all covered with black and disappeared. Then he brought the sun to life again.

Short Bull and Kicking Bear came back bringing us the good news. Now everywhere we are dancing this new dance to roll up the earth, to bring back the dead. A new world is coming.

This Old Unc told me.

Then I saw it myself: the dancing. People were holding each other by the hand, singing, whirling around, looking at the sun. They had a little spruce tree in the middle of the dance circle. They wore special shirts painted with the sun, the moon, the stars, and magpies. They whirled around; they didn't stop dancing.

Some of the dancers fell down in a swoon, as if they were dead. The medicine men fanned them with sweet-smelling cedar smoke and they came to life again They told the people, "We were dead. We went to the moon and the morning star. We found our dead fathers and mothers there, and we talked to them." When they woke up, these people held in their hands star rocks, moon rocks, different kinds of rocks from those we have on this earth. They clutched strange meats from star and moon animals. The dance leader told them not to be afraid of white men who forbade them to dance this *wanagi-wachipi*. They told them that the ghost shirts they wore would not let any white man's bullets through. So they danced; I saw it.

The earth never rolled up. The buffalo never came back, and the dead relatives never came to life again. It was the soldier who came; why, nobody knew. The dance was a peaceful one, harming nobody, but I guess the white people thought it was a war dance.

Many people were afraid of what the soldiers would do. We had no guns any more, and hardly had any horses left. We depended on the white man for everything, yet the whites were afraid of us, just as we were afraid of them.

Then when the news spread that Sitting Bull had been killed at Standing Rock for being with the ghost dancers, the people were really scared. Some of the old people said: "Let's go to Pine Ridge and give ourselves up, because the soldiers won't shoot us if we do. Old Red Cloud will protect us. Also, they're handing out rations up there."

So my father and mother and Old Unc got the buggy and their old horse and drove with us children toward Pine Ridge. It was cold and snowing. It wasn't a happy ride; all the grown-ups were worried. Then the soldiers stopped us. They had big fur coats on, bear coats. They were warm and we were freezing, and I remember wishing I had such a coat. They told us to go no further, to stop and make a camp right there. They told the same thing to everybody who came, by foot, or horse, or buggy. So there was a camp, but little to eat and little firewood, and the soldiers made a ring around us and let nobody leave.

Then suddenly there was a strange noise, maybe four, five miles away, like the tearing of a big blanket, the biggest blanket in the world. As soon as he heard it, Old Unc burst into tears. My old ma started to keen as for the dead, and people were running around, weeping, acting crazy.

I asked Old Unc, "Why is everybody crying?"

He said, "They are killing them, they are killing our people over there! "

My father said, "That noise—that's not the ordinary soldier guns. These are the big wagon guns which tear people to bits—into little pieces!" I could not understand it, but everybody was weeping, and I wept too. Then a day later—or was it two? No, I think it was the next day, we passed by there. Old Unc said: "You children might as well see it; look and remember."

There were dead people all over, mostly women and children, in a ravine near a stream called Chankpe-opi Wakpala, Wounded Knee Creek.

The people were frozen, lying there in all kinds of postures, their motion frozen too. The soldiers, who were stacking up bodies like fire wood, did not like us passing by. They told us to leave there, double-quick or else. Old Unc said: "We'd better do what they say right now, or we'll lie there too."

So we went on toward Pine Ridge, but I had seen. I had seen a dead mother with a dead baby sucking at her breast. The little baby had on a tiny beaded cap with the design of the American flag.

(Quoted from Dick Fool Bull in Erdoes and Ortiz 481–84)

In the 1960s a White River Sioux woman, Jenny Leading Cloud, told an end-of-the-world myth at the center of which is a repre-sentation of the old Indian people.

Sioux: The End of the World

Somewhere at a place where the prairie and the Maka Sicha, the Badlands, meet, there is a hidden cave. Not for a long, long time has anyone been able to find it. Even now, with so many highways, cars, and tourists, no one has discovered this cave.

In it lives a woman so old that her face looks like a shriveled-up walnut. She is dressed in rawhide, the way people used to be before the white man came. She has been sitting there for a thousand years or more, working on a blanket strip for her buffalo robe. She is making the strip out of dyed porcupine quills, the way our ancestors did before white traders brought glass beads to this turtle continent. Resting beside her, licking his paws, watching her all the time is Shunka Sapa, a huge black dog. His eyes never wander from the old woman, whose teeth are worn flat, worn down to little stumps, she has used them to flatten so many porcupine quills.

A few steps from where the old woman sits working on her blanket strip, a huge fire is kept going. She lit this fire a thousand years ago and has kept it alive ever since. Over the fire hangs a big earthen pot, the kind some Indian peoples used to make before the white man came with his kettles of iron. Inside the big pot, wojapi is boiling and bubbling. Wojapi is berry soup, good and sweet and red. That soup has been boiling in the pot for a long time, ever since the fire was lit.

Every now and then the old woman gets up to stir the wojapi in the huge earthen pot. She is so old and feeble that it takes her a while to get up and hobble over to the fire. The moment her back is turned, the huge black dog starts pulling the porcupine quills out of her blanket strip. This way she never makes any progress, and her quillwork remains forever unfinished. The Sioux people used to say that if the old woman ever finishes her blanket strip, then at the very moment that she threads the last porcupine quill to complete the design, the world will come to an end

(Quoted from Jenny Leading Cloud in Erdoes and Ortiz 485–86)

For the Cheyenne, the end centers on the destruction of the world tree, or *axis mundi*, on which the world turns.

Cheyenne: The Tree That Holds Up the World

We don't know where it is anymore, but somewhere in the north there is a great pole, a huge tree trunk like the sun dance pole but bigger. It holds up the world. For a long time, a very long time, the Great White Grandfather Beaver has been gnawing at that pole, and they say he has already gnawed halfway through it. Whenever Grandfather Beaver gets angry at something, he gnaws faster and faster at the pole.

Well, once he gnaws all the way through it, it will fall over and everything is going to crash into a bottomless nothing. It will be the end of everything, the end of the people, the end of ends. So we take care not to make Grandfather Beaver angry. We never eat beaver or touch beaver skins. That way maybe the world will last longer.

(Erdoes and Ortiz 484–85 from Mrs. Medicine Bull)

In the manner of a myth, a Kiowa woman of the twentieth century told of a young woman's poignant vision that occurred at the time the last of the free-ranging buffalo were being wiped out. The life of the Kiowa revolved around the buffalo—it was a source of food, hides for shelter and clothing, and spiritual sustenance. The wild herds began to be depleted soon after the arrival of white men, who hunted them for hides, and they were rendered almost extinct, along with many Plains Indian lifeways, when federal policy called for the buffalo's extermination.

Kiowa: The Mountain Opens for the Buffalos

This was at a time when some of the Kiowas were still free to roam, and they were camped on the north side of Mount Scott. A young woman got up at dawn and watched the mists rising from the creek. Out across the water, through the haze, she saw the last buffalo herd appear. The leader of the herd walked straight for Mount Scott, and the cows, their calves, and a few young males all followed him. These were the only buffalo that had survived.

As the young woman watched, the whole face of the mountain opened up. Inside, there was a world that was green and fresh, the way it once was when the woman had been little. The rivers there were clear, not running red with blood. The wild plums were in bloom, and the redbuds climbed up the slopes. It was a beautiful world inside the mountain, and the buffalos walked into it and were never seen again.

(Marriott, *American* 169–70 from Old Lady Horse [Spear Woman])

For the Pawnee the end comes when the South Star catches the North Star.

Pawnee: The Stars All Fall to Earth

The lord of all things, Tirawa Atius, decides everything that will happen. In the beginning of things, he set a great bull buffalo in the northwestern sky, and each year the bull loses one hair. Each time a hair falls, there is a meteor shower, and as time passes, the sun and moon grow dim. When all the buffalo's hair has fallen out, the world will end.

Also, in the beginning, Tirawa Atius told the North Star and the South Star to look after fate. The North Star talked directly to the Pawnee people, telling them that each year the South Star gets a little closer, moving northward. When it catches up with the North Star, the world will end.

The final destruction of the world is in the hands of the gods of the four directions. The West will issue the command, and the East will obey it. The stars will all fall to earth and become a new race of people, and the people left in the world at this time will fly up into the sky and become stars.

(Bierlein 248)

A Cherokee apocalypse sees the end of this world as the beginning of new one.

Cherokee: Island on the Water

A great island on the water it is, the earth, and it is held up by four pieces of rawhide, one at each of the four directions. The rawhide is attached to a vault of rock crystal high in the heavens. Some day, once the rawhide has grown old, it will crack and break and the earth will fall back into the waters and life will come to an end. Then, just like the last time, the creator will bring the earth back from the waters and recreate the world and life will start again.

(Bierlein 249 from Mooney, Cherokee)

One Hopi vision of the world's end—that of a Bear Clan man of Old Oraibi—contains a new emergence or rebirth into a fifth world. The prophecy is not accepted by all Hopis. It speaks of recent and current events, notably the two World Wars and a third one yet to come. Destruction of the world by nuclear weapons will be almost complete, leaving only the Hopi country as an oasis. Those people of good heart who remain alive will come there and form one people, regardless of color.

The moment is seen as being not far off. It will come with the end of the Hopi ceremonies and will be signaled when a kachina removes his mask during a public dance in the plaza, and when the Blue Star kachina dances in the plaza, indicating the imminent appearance of a distant blue star in the sky.

Hopi: The Fifth World

The emergence into the fifth world has already begun. It has begun with humble people from small nations and tribes. It has begun in the earth itself as well. Seeds are being planted, the same kind as are being planted in the sky as stars. These are the same kind of seeds that are being planted in our hearts. All these seeds are the same, and they make the emergence into the fifth world, which is connected to the three worlds before this one, the fourth world we live in now, the fifth world to which we go, and the worlds beyond even that one.

(Waters 408–409)

Native American versions of the end of the world thus foresee the end of a culture and, in a distant time that is in some sense present time as well, the rebirth of an old life that was never, in fact, dead. This is one more example in Indian mythology of the understanding that myth time is forever and that souls can live in it even as they suffer the realities of "life as we know it."

Part Three
HEROES AND HEROINES

As fascinating as we find gods and goddesses and their creations, it is natural that we relate most directly to myths of human heroes and heroines. Any given hero or heroine in mythology is a reflection of the values and priorities of the culture that gives him form, but he or she also stands as one of many expressions of the larger human persona, as our representative in the dream world that is myth. Joseph Campbell wrote of "the hero with a thousand faces" and applied the term *monomyth* (taken from James Joyce) to what he and others have seen as a universal heroic pattern in which the hero enters the world miraculously, undertakes a quest or undergoes severe trials, often descends to the mysterious and dangerous "other" world—sometimes in search of a father—and returns to his people with a great boon. The pattern is found in fairy tales and legends from all parts of the world, as well as in myth.

Many scholars have noted the possible connection between the hero's quest and the ritual journey of the shaman. Whether he is Jesus, Theseus, the Irish Cuchulainn, or Herakles, the hero who descends to the world of darkness and death resembles the shaman in many cultures who journeys to the spirit world to retrieve a lost or sick tribal member. In the case of some heroes their shamanic sources are clear, and their stories serve as narrative correlatives for rituals. This is particularly true of heroes with shamanlike powers— the ability to cure, for example, or to make magical use of words and music—who literally descend to the underworld to bring back the dead. The myths of Jesus and Orpheus are examples. Jesus raises

Lazarus from the dead, changes water to wine, cures the lame and the blind, and descends to Hell to retrieve lost humanity, represented by Adam and Eve. Orpheus, whose magical music brings about altered states of consciousness, descends to the underworld to attempt the retrieval of his beloved Eurydice. In both cases the activities of these heroes serve as the narrative bases for mysterious rituals of curing or purification.

Whoever the hero(ine) may be, he or she journeys as a metaphor for our own exploration of the unconscious realm in dreams, in prayer, and in various esoteric disciplines. The hero is our representative in the world where our monsters and nightmares are confronted as reality and where our deepest wishes sometimes come true. The myth of the "hero with a thousand faces" is our universal metaphor for the search for self-knowledge as individuals, as cultures, and as a species. To accompany the hero—as we so willingly do in myth and folklore—is to recognize ourselves in what Campbell calls "the wonderful song of the soul's high adventure" (*Hero* 6).

The monomyth of the hero contains many specific elements, but that is not to say that each hero or heroine acts out each one. A comparison of mythic heroes from around the world, however, does reveal a shadow myth—an archetypal pattern—behind the many and very different cultural masks.

The hero is usually miraculously conceived. The Aztec/Toltec Quetzalcoatl is born of a virgin, as are Jesus and the Hindu hero Karna. The Buddha, in the form of a white elephant, conceives himself in his mother's dream. Heroes usually are born during a difficult period, when they are needed. Their miraculous arrival suggests the universal hope for a new beginning—a new injection of the divine into a broken world. By extension, the hero birth can speak not only to the needs and the redemption of a culture but also to individual psychological and spiritual conditions. The hero's conception and birth can represent the beginning of the hero process within us—what Carl Jung and others have called the process of

146

individuation by which we undertake a shamanic journey into our own unknown in order to retrieve our lost selves. To do this we must discover the relationship between ourselves and the larger order of things—what in myth is the supreme being or, in patriarchal cultures, the "father" for whom heroes so often search.

As for the virgin who gives birth to the hero, she is the earthly context—the great goddess or the mother of us all, sometimes the earth herself. She is the physical existence in which we must carry the divine energy represented by the sometimes mysterious and unapproachable father. The hero is engendered by that intangible energy, but to be alive in this world he or she must be born of a flesh-and-blood mother, the vessel of life without whom the divine cannot become human.

More often than not, the young hero is threatened by the forces of evil in the world. The longing for a new beginning in the life of a culture or an individual is always confronted by the forces of the status quo, those who abandon the child in the wilderness, try to kill him in his crib, chop him into pieces, or place him in a basket and leave him to the river's flow. In terms of the personal journey, the newborn hero within is a threat to our sense of emotional safety; it is often easiest simply to smother him.

The central events in the heroic life, as in our own, center around the quest—the search for fulfillment. In many cases the specific goal is the welfare of the hero's people, represented variously as the Kingdom of God, enlightenment, a new crop. The quest is always marked by trials—monsters to overcome, impossible tasks to achieve. The trials and tasks reflect the realities of the given culture. For many patriarchal heroes the worst and most powerful "monster" is that of female sexuality represented by an enchantress or femme fatale: Circe, Delilah, and the Sirens are all examples. In cultures that emphasize the dualities—light and dark, good and evil—there is frequently an arch monster, Satan or some other representative of absolute evil.

At some point in the hero quest there is usually a confrontation with the ultimate nemesis, death itself. To defeat this force, either

147

physically or spiritually, the hero must descend to the Land of the Dead. Culturally and individually the hero's descent leads us to a realization of our mortality, and through his return from the dead he helps us to achieve power over that mortality. The hero teaches us that only by facing the monsters within can we achieve wholeness. So it is that the hero returns from the Land of the Dead and brings a gift from the unknown. It might be spiritual knowledge or it might be wheat or corn.

In Native America heroes take several forms. We have already seen examples of the culture hero who is in some sense divine, often a creator or transformer and sometimes a trickster. The culture hero usually arrives after the creation, transforms inanimate objects into living ones, and alters the shape of nature. He also teaches the people how to survive. Culture heroes give a particular lifestyle, a particular identity, to individual culture groups. In this sense, Raven and Coyote are culture heroes in many of the creation and trickster myths we have considered above; and gods and goddesses, characters like White Buffalo Woman, Spider Woman, the Acoma sisters, the Great Hare, and Glooscap, are also culture heroes. Spider Woman teaches weaving, the many twin gods of the Southwest kill monsters, and several culture heroes steal fire for humans. Culture heroes also teach the people about death and how to cope with it ritually.

Heroes

More often than not, American Indian heroes are male. The same can be said of the mythologies of Greece, Egypt, Sumer, India, or any other part of the world where such activities as the quest, the hunt, and the struggle with enemies are primarily associated with the male.

The Culture Hero

"Dug from the Ground" or "Lost Across the Ocean" is a transformer culture-hero myth of the Hupa Indians, an inland tribe of northern California. This myth, told by a Hupa Indian, contains the monomyth elements of the miraculous birth, the voyage to the other world, and the tests.

Hupa: Dug from the Ground

An old woman was living with her granddaughter, a virgin. The girl used to go to dig roots and her grandmother used to say to her, "You must not dig those with two stocks." The girl wondered why she was always told that. One morning she thought, "I am going to dig one," so she went across the river and began digging. She thought, "I am going to take out one with a double stock." When she had dug it out she heard a baby cry. She ran back to the river, and when she got there she heard someone crying "mother" after her. She jumped into the boat and pushed it across. When she got across, the baby had tumbled down to the other shore. She ran up to the house and there she heard it crying on that side. She ran into the house, then she heard it crying back of the house. At once she sat down and then she heard it tumble on the roof of the house. The baby tumbled through the smoke-hole and then rolled about on the floor. The old woman jumped up and put it in a baby basket. The young woman sat with her back to the fire and never looked at the child.

The old woman took care of the baby alone. After a time it commenced to sit up and finally to walk. When he was big enough to shoot, the old woman made a bow and he began to kill birds. Afterward he killed all kinds of game; and, because his mother never looked at him, he gave whatever he killed to his grandmother. Finally he became a man. The young woman had been in the habit of going out at dawn and not returning until dark. She brought back with her acorns as long as her finger. One time the young man

149

thought "I am going to watch and see where she goes." The young woman had always said to herself, "If he will bring acorns from the place I bring them, and if he will kill a white deer, I will call him my son." Early one morning the son saw his mother come out of the house and start up the ridge. He followed her and saw her go along until she came to a dry tree. She climbed this and it grew with her to the sky. The young man then returned saying, "Tomorrow I am going up there." The woman came home at night with the usual load of long acorns.

The next morning the man went the way his mother had gone, climbed the tree as he had seen her do, and it grew with him to the sky. When he arrived there he saw a road. He followed that until he came to an oak, which he climbed, and waited to see what would happen. Soon he heard laughing girls approaching. They came to the tree and began to pick acorns from allotted spaces under it. The young man began to throw down acorns. "That's right, Bluejay," said one of the girls. Then another said, "It might be Dug-from-the ground. You can hardly look at him, they say, he is so handsome." Two others said, "Oh, I can look at him, I always look at this walking one (pointing to the sun); that is the one you can hardly look at." He came down from the tree and passed between the girls. The two who had boasted they could look at him, turned their faces to the ground. The other two who had thought they could not look him in the face were able to do so.

The young man killed the deer, the killing of which the mother had made the second condition for his recognition as a son. He then filled the basket from his mother's place under the tree and went home. When the woman saw him with the acorns as long as one's finger, she called him her son.

After a time he said, "I am going visiting." "All right," said the grandmother, and then she made for him a bow and arrows of blue-stone, and a shinny stick and sweat-house wood of the same material. These he took and concealed by putting them under the muscles of his forearm. He dressed himself for the journey and set out. He went to the home of the immortals at the edge of the world toward the east. When he got down to the shore on this side they saw him. One of them took out the canoe of red obsidian and stretched it until it was the proper size. He launched it and came across for him. When he had landed, the young man placed his hand on the bow and as he did so, the boat gave a creak, he was so strong. When they had crossed he went to the village. In the middle of it he saw a house of blue-stone with a pavement in front of black obsidian. He went in and heard one say, "It is my son-in-law for whom I had expected to be a long time looking."

When the sun had set there came back from different places ten brothers. Some had been playing kiñ, some had been playing shinny, some had been hunting, some spearing salmon, and others had been shooting at a mark. Eagle and Panther were both married to daughters of the family. They said to him, "You here, brother-in law?" "Yes," he said, "I came a little while ago." When it was supper time they put in front of him a basket of money's meat, which mortal man cannot swallow. He ate two baskets of it and they thought he must be a smart man. After they had finished supper they all went to the sweat-house to spend the night. At midnight the young man went to the river to swim. There he heard a voice say, "The sweat-house wood is all gone." Then Mink told him that men could not find sweat-house wood near by, but that some was to be found to the southeast. They called to him for wood from ten sweat-houses and he said "Yes" to all. Mink told him about everything they would ask him to do. He went back to the sweat-house and went in. When the east whitened with the dawn, he went for sweat-house wood as they had told him. He came to the place where the trail forks and one of them turns to the northeast and the other to the southeast. There he drew out from his arm the wood his grandmother had provided him with and split it fine. He made this into ten bundles and carried them back to the village. When he got there he put them down carefully but the whole earth shook with the shock. He carried a bundle to each sweat-house. They all sweated themselves. He spent the day there and at evening went again to the sweat-house. When he went to the river to swim, Mink met him again and told him that the next day they would play shinny.

After they were through breakfast the next morning, they said, "Come, brother-in-law, let us go to the place where they play shinny." They all went and after placing their bets began to play. Twice they were beaten. Then

151

they said "Come, brother-in-law, play." They passed him a stick. He pressed down on it and broke it. "Let me pick up something," he said. He turned about and drew out his concealed shinny stick and the balls. Then he stepped out to play and Wildcat came to play against him. The visitor made the stroke and the balls fell very near the goal. Then he caught Wildcat smashing his face into its present shape, and threw the ball over the line. He played again, this time with Fox. Again he made the stroke and when he caught Fox he pinched his face out long as it has been ever since. He then struck the ball over the line and won. The next time he played against Earthquake. The ground opened up a chasm but he jumped over it. Earthquake threw up a wall of blue-stone but he threw the ball through it. "Dol" it rang as it went through. Then he played with Thunder. It rained and there was thunder. It was the running of that one which made the noise. It was then night and he had won back all they had lost. There were ten strings of money, besides otterskins, fisherskins, and blankets.

The next day they went to shoot at the white bird which Indians can never hit. The others commenced to shoot and then they said to their guest, " Come, you better shoot." They gave him a bow, which broke when he drew it. Then he pulled out his own and said, " I will shoot with this although the nock has been cut down and it is not very good." They thought, "He can't hit anything with that." He shot and hit the bird, and dentalia fell all about. They gathered up the money and carried it home.

The Hupa man went home to his grandmother. As many nights as it seemed to him he had spent, so many years he had really been away. He found his grandmother lying by the fire. Both of the women had been worried about him. He said to them, "I have come back for you." "Yes," they said, "we will go." Then he repaired the house, tying it up anew with hazel withes. He poked a stick under it and away it went to the end of the world toward the east, where he had married. They are living there yet.

(Quoted from Goddard 146)

Other Indian heroes are more clearly human, even when they are conceived through some divine agency. Often their myths are related to specific rituals or tribal practices. Several heroes are vision questers who successfully achieve divine tasks and bring divine gifts to their people. Many are warriors; some of these are recent additions to mythology, arising out of heroic deeds of real Indians in the wars against European intruders. Many of the Indian heroes are expressions of agricultural and hunting priorities; they learn from Animal Masters, or Mistresses, the proper way to hunt, or they learn from divine spirits the secrets of planting.

The Iroquois Seneca tell of their Corn Mother, who was impregnated by Turtle, the personification of the foundation on which the original mother landed when she fell from the sky at the original earth-diver creation. After her death and before she gave birth to the twins, corn grew from the Corn Mother's breasts. When the corn was ripe the twins' grandmother gave them each an ear of it as instructed by her daughter.

The Twins

Twins are an important motif in many parts of the world—especially in connection with creation myths and solar-lunar mythology. Generally they stand for the great dualities of nature—especially good and evil. In Hinduism there are the twins Manu and Yemo, in Zoroastrianism Ohrmazd and Ahriman. Twins also exist in the myths of Greece and Rome and those of the Dogon people in Africa, to mention only a few examples. Twins are a favorite motif in Native American mythology as well. Sometimes they are fathered by the sun—especially in the Southwest—and sometimes by the original culture hero. In either case they usually do some of the work of creation. Often—especially among the northern tribes—the mother of the twins dies at their birth. In many cases the twins go in search of their divine father. While it is true that the twins sometimes reflect the duality of the world, it must be said that in many Indian cultures they simply represent the existence of two moieties, or socioreligious subdivisions, in the tribe. Even when one twin is clearly better than the other, the lesser twin still seems to have a valid role in the creative process.

Some of the better-known twins or, when not technically twins, twin figures among the Native Americans are the Navajo Nayenez-gani and Tobadzhistshini (Monster Slayer and Born for Water), who are children of Changing Woman and the Sun; the sisters Iatiku and Nautsiti, who, as we have seen, nurture the Keresan Pueblos; and the Seneca Hadentheni and Hanigongendatha (He Who Speaks and He Who Interprets). The myth of the Navajo Twins, contained mostly in the Monsterway section of the Blessingway, contains the familiar themes of miraculous conception and birth, the trials or tests—including the slaying of monsters—and the quest involving, above all, the search for the father. The Navajo Twins are culture heroes in that they bring back knowledge to their people.

Navajo: The Deeds of the Twins

Even in this new world, however, which some call the Glittering World, echoes of the old world haunted the people. A number of women who had abused themselves with cacti and other objects when the men and women had lived separately began to give birth. In each case they bore monstrous offspring, which were abandoned in the hopes they would die. But they didn't. Instead, they grew up to be enemies and destroyers, lurking here and there, and giving the people reason to live every day in fear. There was Big Monster who lived on Mount Taylor; the Bird Monsters on Shiprock, the Monster That Kicked People Off the Cliff; the Monster That Killed with His Eyes, Horned Monster, and many, many others.

Before too long, the monsters had devoured everyone but First Man and First Woman and four other people. First Man hoped that the gods would help them, but First Woman doubted it, saying that they didn't yet know what pleased or displeased the gods. One morning, First Man noticed that a dark cloud covered the crest of the mountain called Gobernador Knob today. First Man decided to investigate, saying that he would protect himself by surrounding himself with songs. Just as he got to the peak, amid lightning, thunder, and driving rain, he heard an infant cry. Finding the spot despite the storms, he discovered a small piece of turquoise in the form of a female, which he took down the mountain to First Woman.

In an elaborate ceremony, the Holy People created a female baby from the turquoise figure, and this would become Changing Woman. When she came of age, reaching puberty, a ceremony was held so that she would be able to bear children. Called Kinaalda to this day [see Part One, page 33, above], the ceremony was held on Gobernador Knob. The rite included the dressing of Changing Woman in while beads, having her run four times in the direction of the rising sun, and the singing by Talking God of twelve songs called hogan songs

Sometime after the ceremony, Changing Woman grew lonely and wandered off. She lay down on a flat rock near a waterfall with her feet facing the east and felt the warmth of the sun come over her and fill her. In time, she gave birth to twin boys. They would come to be known as Monster Slayer and Child Born of Water. As the boys grew older, they were repeatedly challenged to races by Talking God. Encouraged by Nilch'i, the Wind, they eventually grew strong enough and fast enough to outrun the god (who was extremely pleased). Meanwhile, the twins wondered who their father was and continually asked their mother, Changing Woman, but she wouldn't tell them, only saying that he was dangerous.

The monsters were also still dangerous. One day a monster approached Changing Woman's house and demanded that she give him her sons to eat. She explained that she had no sons, that the tracks the monster saw on the ground were tracks she had made with her hand to pretend that there were people around and lessen her feelings of loneliness. The monster was satisfied and left. On another occasion, when the house was entirely surrounded by monsters, the Wind blew up a gale around it big enough to protect the people inside. Changing Woman feared greatly for her sons, but they continued to go out exploring during the day.

One day the sons came upon a column of smoke rising from a hole in the ground. Peering down, they discovered Spider Woman. Invited in, the boys were ashamed, because they could not explain exactly who they were, not knowing who their father was. Spider Woman told them that he was the sun, and lived far above in the sky, and that the way to his house was dangerous. To get there one had to pass through the rocks that crush travelers, reeds that cut them to pieces, cacti that tear them, and boiling sands that turn them to ashes. But, Spider Woman said, she would tell them how to make the journey and give them charms and protection that would see them through the ordeal. She would also teach them how to pass the tests that their father would subject them to, for he would not be happy to see them. After surviving the obstacles in their long journey, the twins reached the sun's house to find him out. They told the sun's wife that they had come to see their father. The sun's wife was angry that her husband had not been keeping his distance from other women, but she kept silent and agreed to hide the twins when the sun came home at the end of his day's labor. As he settled down, his wife revealed the two hiding boys and demanded, ''Whose sons are these?''

Before the sun could answer, the twins explained that they had made a long journey to see their father. But the sun would not believe they were children of his until they passed several ordeals. He made them smoke tobacco that could kill, eat cornmeal that was poisoned, and endure a killingly hot sweat bath, as well as flinging them against a wall of sharp flints. Protected by Spider Woman's magic, they survived all this unharmed and the sun was convinced. He offered them their pick of corn and plants, wild animals, domesticated animals, precious jewels, but the twins told the sun about the monsters, saying that they would like all those gifts later, but now they needed weapons.

The sun was at first reluctant, because some of the monsters were also his offspring, but eventually he let the twins take two kinds of lightning, suited them in armor made of flint, and sent them back to the world on a stroke of lighting. Their first challenge was the Big Giant, who dwelled near Mount Taylor and was known to go to Hot Springs to drink from a great lake there. The twins laid in wait at the lake and in due course the Big Giant arrived and spotted them. They exchanged taunting insults with the vast monster, who then threw four lightning bolts in succession, but each one missed, thanks to the protection given the twine by Spider Woman, or, some say, thanks to the Wind. At that point, a brilliant bolt of lightning came out of the sky from where the sun's disk shone, stunning the Big

Monster. Throwing their own bolts, the twins killed the giant. They severed the Big Monster's head and his blood gushed into the valley in a torrent, which the twins succeeded in stemming by cutting a line across the valley with a stone knife. The giant's blood congealed into a solid black mass, filling the valley below Mount Taylor, and can be seen there today as what the white man calls lava.

Thereafter, the older twin, called Monster Slayer, took on the task of killing the other monsters, often aided by his brother along with chipmunks, ground squirrels, and other animals. He slew the Horned Monster; the Bird Monsters, the Monster Who Kicks People Off the Cliff, and all the other especially dangerous ones. That task over, the twins came across another group of monsters living in a room below the ground. These were Hunger, Poverty, Sleep, Lice Man, and Old Age. The twins threatened to kill them, but each in turn persuaded the warriors to spare him. Hunger said he was necessary to keep people eating, planting, and hunting. Without him, Poverty argued, clothes and moccasins would not wear out, and people would not make new and better ones. Sleep claimed to be necessary when anyone is ill or tired. Everyone knows that lice get in people's hair if they do not stay clean, and Lice Man offered himself as a good reminder. And without him, reasoned Old Age, there would not be room for new people on the earth. So the twins spared all these monsters.

Then they traveled to the four sacred mountains from which they could see that there were no more monsters to be slain. There was now order and harmony in the world. Later, the sun joined them to discuss the disposal of the monsters' corpses and it was agreed that they should all be buried under the blood of the Big Giant at Mount Taylor. Occasionally today, one may see a few bits and pieces protruding from the rocks—a claw or a finger that was chopped off—and imagine that they are fossils. The sun then left, taking his weapons and armor, and leaving word that he would like Changing Woman to meet him five days hence at Gobernador Knob.

On the appointed day, the sun came to Changing Woman and asked her to come with him to the west, where he would establish a home for her;

so that they could be together at the end of his daily labors. But she would have nothing to do with him. He tried to persuade her: "What use is male without female? What use is female without male? What use are we two without one another?"

After a long silence, Changing Woman explained that she would want a beautiful house, "floating on the shimmering water," with gems and animals all around her. And when the sun asked why she made such demands, she said, "You are of the sky and I am of the earth. You are constant in your brightness, but I must change with the seasons." And she said, "Remember, as different as we are, you and I, we are of one spirit. As dissimilar as we are, you and I, we are of equal worth. As unlike as you and I are there must always be solidarity between the two of us. Unlike each other as you and I are, there can be no harmony in the universe as long as there is no harmony between us. If there is to be such harmony, my requests must matter to you."

So it was agreed, and Changing Woman went to live in the west beyond the farthest shore, joined each evening by the sun. The twins went to live where two rivers join in the valley of the San Juan. And after summer rain, when the mist clears, the bright colors of a rainbow shimmer in the moist light and the forms of the twins appear to this day.

(Quoted from Page and Page, *Navajo* 31–33)

The Quest

The myth of the Blackfoot hero Kutoyis (Blood Clot) is a particularly comprehensive expression of the hero monomyth. It contains the miraculous conception and birth, the slaying of monsters, the challenge of evil women, the descent to a kind of underworld, the sacrificial death and rebirth theme, and several other archetypal motifs, including especially the hero journey or quest. The emphasis on the number four—four arrowheads, four arrows to kill the old man, four ritual meals of man's flesh—suggests the role of Kutoyis as a world hero of the four directions, of *all* the people. His resurrection reminds us of that of the Master Bear in the Cherokee myth of Bear Man.

Blackfoot: The Hero Kutoyis (Blood Clot)

Down where those two creeks meet, a man once lived with his wife and two daughters in comfort, enjoying the fruits of the land and the hunt. But the man was getting to be old, so he was delighted when one day a young man came to his camp, a brave man and a great hunter. He gave the young man his two daughters as wives and all his wealth except for a small lodge in which he and his wife lived.

The grateful son-in-law would hunt and share the meat with the old couple and give them skin to make robes from and to sleep on. The young man was so skilled as a hunter that before long he had managed to collect a whole herd of buffalo, which he kept under a big logjam where the two creeks met. Whenever the hunter needed some buffalo meat or a hide, he would get the old man to come to the logjam. The old man would jump on it until the frightened buffalo ran out, and the hunter would shoot one or two—never killing wastefully.

As the months went by, the hunter stopped giving the old man any of the meat. He and his wife were hungry all the time, growing thin and weak. The hunter still made the old man help in the hunt by stomping on the logjam, then sent him home empty-handed. Lest the old man's daughters take pity on their parents, he instructed them never to give the old people anything.

This was fine with the older daughter, who had grown just as mean as her husband, but the younger daughter was different. She stole some meat and, when no one was looking, threw it into her parents' lodge. In this way the old couple was sustained for a little while longer.

One day the young hunter summoned the old man for his chore at the logjam. He stomped, the buffalo ran out, and the hunter shot one of them, but only wounded it. The buffalo ran off, but finally fell over dead. The old man followed it and came to a place where the buffalo had lost a large clot of blood.

Pretending to stumble and fall, the old man let his arrows fall from his quiver, and as he picked them up he also stuffed the blood clot into the quiver.

His son-in-law came running up. "What is that you're picking up there?" he demanded.

"Nothing. I fell down and spilled my bow and arrows."

"Curse you, you lazy old good-for-nothing," the son-in-law said, snatching the old man's bow and arrows from his quiver. "Go home."

The old man hurried back to his lodge and told his wife to put the kettle on. The old woman was pleased to think that their son-in-law had turned generous, but the old man told her it wasn't that way. When the water reached a boil, the old man tipped his quiver over the kettle and immediately there came the sound of a child crying in pain.

The old couple looked in the kettle and were amazed to see a little boy in the water. They pulled him out and quickly made a cradleboard for him, tying him in. Then they talked. If their son-in-law found out it was a boy, he would surely kill it. But if he thought it was a girl, he would think that one day he would have another wife. So they decided to tell their daughters and their husband that they had a little girl. They named it Kutoyis, which means clot of blood.

When the hunter and his two wives came home that day, they heard an infant crying, so the hunter sent his younger wife over to see what had happened. She returned, saying that her parents had given birth to a girl child. He didn't believe her, so he sent his older wife. She came back saying the same thing, so he believed her. Thinking he would someday add another wife to his lodge, he told his wives to take some pemmican over to the old people from now on so there would be plenty of milk for the growing child.

On the fourth day the child spoke, telling the old woman to tie him in turn to each of the four lodgepoles. "When I am at the fourth, I will fall out and grow up." She did so, and at each pole he seemed to grow some. They tied him to the last pole and he fell out, a grown man. "Well," he said, "there doesn't seem to be much food around here. I see they have quite a lot of it over at the other lodge." The old woman became terrified. "Be quiet, they'll hear you and he'll kill us," she cried. "They don't give us food." Then the old man explained to Kutoyis how they had been mistreated by their son-in-law—how he had taken their arrows and starved them. He did, however, still have four stone arrowheads. So the old man and Kutoyis made a new bow and four new arrows, to which they attached the arrowheads.

"Come now, father," said Kutoyis early the next morning. "We will go and kill a buffalo for food." The two men made their way to the son-in-law's logjam and the old man pounded on it. A fat buffalo came out and Kutoyis killed it.

Now the son-in-law appeared and, on finding the old man already skinning a buffalo, he cried out, "Take a good breath old man, for it'll be your last one." But Kutoyis, who was hiding behind the carcass, told the old man what to say. "Maybe the last breath will be yours," the old man shouted at his son-in-law. At this, the enraged son-in-law shot at the old man but missed, and the old man shot back and missed, too. After three more misses on each side, Kutoyis stood up and challenged the son-in-law and promptly shot and killed him with four arrows. He then went to the man's lodge and killed his two wives, giving the lodge and all its food supplies to the old couple.

"Now I must make my journey," said Kutoyis. "Tell me where there are people." The old man directed him to Badger Creek, where there were many lodges, and Kutoyis went there. In the center of the settlement was a fine lodge with a bear figure painted on it. But Kutoyis chose to go to another lodge where there were two old women. They gave Kutoyis some dried meat to eat and told him about the Great Bear chief who mistreated the people of his village, keeping all the best food for himself. Kutoyis went to the place where the chief's buffalo were kept, killed a fat calf, and told the women to hang the best pieces to dry outside of their lodge. When the bear people and their chief came to claim the good meat, Kutoyis killed them all—all, that is, but a young female, whom he left alone to breed new bears in the forest. Having rid these people of a monster, Kutoyis went on to find more people.

He found a camp on Sun River and went into the lodge of an old woman. Once again he was given bad food and was told of the tyranny of the village chief, the Great Snake, and his snake followers. Kutoyis cut these oppressors to pieces, sparing only a young female to go and breed new snakes in the forest.

161

The villagers told Kutoyis about the monster Ai-sin-o-ko-ki (Wind Sucker), who lived in the mountains terrorizing the people there. Kutoyis found the horrible monster and looking into his wide-open mouth confronted a scene that disgusted him: there were many people—some only bones, some more recently dead, some barely alive, and some but recently swallowed. Kutoyis leapt into the mouth to help the people. "What is that thing hanging from the ceiling?" he asked them. "It is the monster's heart," they answered. "Then we shall have a ghost dance," the hero announced, "and I shall wear a knife on my head." The people danced around Kutoyis, who himself danced wildly so that at each leap the knife on his head pierced Wind Sucker's heart until he died. Now Kutoyis freed the people who were still alive.

"I must see all the people," said Kutoyis. "Where are there more?" Directed toward a camp up a nearby river, the hero was warned to avoid a woman along the way who challenged all passersby to a wrestling match that always ended in the visitor's death. But Kutoyis knew now that his role in life was to rid the people of evil and to restore harmony in the world, so he went directly to the bad woman's lodge. When he arrived the woman challenged him, but three times he refused, before accepting the fourth call. He noticed that the woman had hidden sharp objects in the grass and realized that she won her matches by throwing her adversaries onto them. Kutoyis turned the tables by throwing the woman there, and she was cut into shreds.

So the great Kutoyis went on. He killed a wicked witch—a woman who tricked people into tripping over a rope and falling to their death into a lake inhabited by a man-eating fish—and eventually he came to the camp of the worst monster of all, the Man Eater.

Here he did something very strange. He told a little girl in the camp that he planned to enter Man Eater's lodge to be eaten. He instructed her to retrieve one of his bones after the meal was done, throw them to the dogs, and cry out, "Kutoyis, the dogs have your bones."

Kutoyis entered the lodge. The fat young man there cut his throat, put him into the kettle to cook, and then ate him. As he was so contented with his meal, Man Eater willingly gave Kutoyis's bones to the little girl when she asked for them. When she threw them to the dogs and called out as the hero had instructed, a miracle took place. Kutoyis rose from the pile of bones and returned to Man Eater's lodge to be eaten again. After being killed, cooked, eaten, and resurrected four times, Kutoyis entered the lodge and killed Man Eater and his wives and children, thus completing the process by which he rid the world of evil.

(Leeming and Page, *God* 90–92; Grinnell, *Blackfoot* 29–38)

The Search for the Father

Some of the Tewa Indians of the New Mexico pueblos recount the myth of Water Jar Boy, born miraculously of a virgin. Water Jar Boy searches for his father and in the process descends to another world.

Tewa: Water Jar Boy

A woman at Sikyatki had a beautiful daughter who refused to get married. The mother spent her days making water jars, and one day she asked the daughter to help mix some clay while she went for water. The girl put some clay on a flat stone and stepped on it, and somehow some of the clay entered her, making her pregnant.

He mother was angry to hear about this, and when she looked again, she saw that her daughter had given birth not to a regular child but to a water jar. Her father came in and said he was glad, especially when he found out the baby was a water jar. He liked the water jar and watched it grow.

In twenty days it was big enough to run around with the other children, and they came to like it, finding out that he was Water Jar Boy. His mother cried all the time because Water Jar Boy had no arms or legs, just a mouth they could feed him by.

Later Water Jar Boy begged to go rabbit hunting, but his grandfather said he couldn't, not without any arms or legs. But the boy pleaded and his grandfather took him. He was rolling along under the mesa when he saw a rabbit and rolled after it, fetching up against a rock, where he broke. Up jumped a boy, glad his old skin was broken. He was a fine-looking boy,

163

handsomely dressed, with a lot of turquoise beads around his neck. He was fleet of foot and that day killed four rabbits before he went to the foot of the mesa to meet his grandfather.

"Who are you?" the old man asked, and he didn't believe it when the handsome boy said he was his grandson. But when he explained what had happened, the old man accepted the boy and they went home. When they got there, his mother thought her father had come back with a handsome suitor, but they explained that it was her son, Water Jar Boy.

Her son went off with the other boys, but one day he came and asked who his father was.

"I don't know," his mother said.

"Well, I'm going to go find him."

"You can't," his mother said. "I've never been with a man, so there isn't anywhere you can look."

"I know where he lives," Water Jar Boy said, and he left, walking southwest toward Horse Mesa Point. There he came to a spring. An old man was walking near the spring and asked the boy where he was going.

"To the spring, to see my father."

"You'll never find your father," the old man said, but the boy insisted he would find him.

"Who is your father?" the man asked, and the boy said, "I think you are."

The man glared at the boy, trying to scare him, but the boy kept on saying, "You are my father." Finally the man put his arms around the boy and said he was glad, and he took him down into the spring. There he saw all his father's relatives and they all ran up and put their arms around him. He stayed with them one night, and then he went home the next day and told his mother what had happened.

Soon his mother got sick and died, and the boy thought there was no reason to stay there alone, so he went back to the spring. There he found his mother with all the other women. His father told him he didn't want the boy living over at Sikyatki, so he had made his mother die and come over to the spring to live. So they all lived together there.

(Coffin 99–101)

The Wicked Parent

The Athabascans of the Subarctic region of the Canadian Northwest Coast followed the tradition common to many Indians of sending boys out on vision quests at puberty. In the vision quest the boy becomes the hero in search of a spirit guide and, therefore, of his destiny. The hero in this Beaver Indian myth from Canada is the boy Swan, a transformer who is much like the ancient tricksters, but one who faces a problem that will be eerily familiar to readers of many stepmother fairy tales and the Greek myth of Phaedra, Hippolytus, and Theseus.

Beaver: Swan

He was Swan, a boy old enough to hunt rabbits now that he had reached puberty. He planned to go rabbit hunting, and his stepmother insisted on going with him. The first rabbit he shot she grabbed and placed between her thighs, where its paws scratched her in its final throes. Later, back home, she lied to her husband, saying that it was Swan who had scratched her when he was molesting her.

Swan's father was furious and made Swan come with him to a distant island, where he abandoned him. Swan cried himself to sleep, but heard a voice in his dreams. It told him to spread pitch around on the rocks. When he woke up, he did this, and soon game birds came and landed on the rocks and were stuck there. That way Swan had plenty to eat all through the winter.

In the spring his father came to the island to gather up his son's bones, but Swan took the canoe and paddled off, leaving the father stranded. Back home Swan loosed an arrow at his stepmother, who fled into the sea to escape. But the arrow was hot, boiling the water, and all the flesh boiled off the wicked woman.

Then Swan took the name of the sun and the moon and traveled the rim of the world, killing the monsters that lurked there, turning them into

165

the animals we have today. When he was done, he made himself into a stone. When the present world comes to an end, he will come back and set things right, they say.

(Bierhorst, *Mythology* 69–70 from Ridington)

Monster-Slayer Trickster

A primary purpose of the hero in all cultures is to destroy monsters who threaten the tribe. We see this in the Blackfoot myth of Kutoyis, for instance. We find it also in the life and name of the Navajo hero Monster Slayer. In this myth of the northeast-coast Passamaquoddy, Micmac, and Maliseet we are reintroduced to the familiar trickster-transformer culture hero Glooscap in his monster-slaying role.

Passamaquoddy, Micmac, Maliseet: Glooscap Slays the Monster

Glooscap had made everything—all the animals just the right size—and he had made a village and taught the people everything they needed to know. Then, as was his custom, he went off into the clouds in his white canoe. All was well in the village; there was a fine spring that flowed with pure water, plenty of hunting and fishing, and children respected their elders.

Then one time the spring dried up. The people wondered what they should do. They knew they couldn't live without water. So they met in council and decided to send a man north to find the source of the spring and find out why it had dried up. This man walked and walked until he came to another village where the water widened out, but it smelled bad and was a sickly yellow color. The man asked for some of the water, even though it was bad, and the people there said they couldn't let him have any.

"You have to get permission from our chief. He lives upstream and he wants to keep all the water for himself."

The man walked on and came across the chief—a fearsome sight. He was a huge monster, so tall he couldn't see his head. He filled the entire valley and had dug a big hole, damming up the water so it wouldn't run. The water itself was foul and poisonous, lying greasily under stinking mist.

The monster chief grinned, a huge horrid grin. His eyes were dull, and he had warts as big as mountains.

"What do you want?" he snarled at the man.

"I came for some water," the man said. "The spring ran dry in our village because you're keeping it all here. We would like some, and we'd be grateful if you wouldn't muddy it up like this."

The monster blinked, and he roared at the man, telling him he didn't care at all about the people. Inside his mouth, the man could see all the things the monster had killed and eaten, and with the monster smacking his lips, the man lost his nerve and ran off. Back home he told everyone that nothing could be done. If they complained, the monster might eat them.

Well, Glooscap was off in his canoe, but he saw all this and said to himself that he would have to get some water for the people. So he painted his body, put hundreds of eagle feathers in his hair, painted himself, made his mouth into a snarl, and stamped his feet. The earth shook, and Glooscap uttered a loud war cry that echoed back and forth from the mountains. He took one of the mountains in his hand, one made entirely of flint, and turned it into a great sharp knife. Thus armed for war, he strode forth amid thunder and lightning and went to where the monster was.

"I want clean water for the people and I will take it now," he said.

The monster shrieked out that the water was his, all his, and he would kill this upstart.

"We'll see about that, you slimy pile of filth," Glooscap cried out. They began to fight and the earth trembled and split open. The ground burst into flames, and forests were shaken into splinters. The monster opened its vast mouth to swallow his assailant, but Glooscap sliced open his vast belly and from it a mighty stream gushed forth, a huge rolling river, flowing past the village and down to the sea.

Seeing that the river was enough water for the people, he grabbed the monster and squeezed it in his hands, and threw it aside, in a swamp, where it became a bullfrog.

(Erdoes and Ortiz 181–84 from Indian sources)

Métis do not constitute a tribe per se; they are mixed-bloods who are partly Indian and partly of European descent. In the following monster-slaying hero myth, the hero, as in many European folktales, does not on the surface appear to be heroic. The story is told by Jean Desjarlais, a Canadian Métis man also called Oohosis, the Messenger Owl.

Métis: Little-Man-with-Hair-All-Over

Little-Man was hairier than a skunk. Hair grew out of his nose and nostrils. He had thick, matted hair between his buttocks. He was not particularly good-looking and he smelled as if he didn't wash often, but he was a merry fellow who laughted a lot, and he never had any trouble finding pretty girls to share his blanket. He was always on the move, eager to discover new things.

Little-Man-with-Hair-All-Over was small, but he succeeded in everything he did. He was tough in a fight, so they called for him whenever there was something dangerous to do. When a bear monster went on a rampage, ripping up lodges with his huge claws and eating the people inside, Little-Man-with-Hair-All-Over had no trouble killing it. For this his grateful people gave him a magic knife.

One time when Little-Man was traveling, he met two brothers and asked what they were up to. "We're looking for adventure," they answered.

"That's exactly what I'm doing. Let's join up and travel together," said Little-Man. "What do they call you?"

"My name is Smoking Mountain," said one. "I'm the oldest. This one here is Broken War Club."

The three wandered on together and after a while came to a fine, large lodge with plenty of buffalo robes lying around. Outside there were racks with jerk meat, and someone had left a large cooking kettle. But the lodge was deserted; there was no trace of any human beings.

"I like this place," said Little-Man. "Let's stay a while."

"Somebody must own it," said Smoking Mountain.

"Well," said Little-Man, "if someone comes and claims it, I won't mind; and if nobody shows up I won't mind either." So they stayed.

Little-Man said to Smoking Mountain: "Let's go hunting. Broken War Club can stay and cook some of that jerk meat for supper." So the two of them took their bows and arrows and went.

But when the hunters came back to camp, there was no supper. Broken War Club was lying under a buffalo robe moaning and groaning.

"What's the matter with you?" asked Little-Man. "You look as if you've been in a fight."

"I'm too embarrassed to tell," answered Broken War Club.

"Suit yourself," said Little-Man, and they ate some cold jerk meat.

The next day Little-Man-with-Hair-All-Over said to Broken War Club: "Let's go out and hunt. Smoking Mountain can stay here and cook." But when the two came back, they found Smoking Mountain also lying under a buffalo robe moaning and groaning. "What happened to you, friend?" asked Little-Man. "You look as if you've been in a fight."

"I'm too ashamed to tell," answered Smoking Mountain.

"You two are some fine cooks!" remarked Little-Man. Again they ate their jerk meat cold.

The next morning Little-Man told the brothers: "You go out and hunt; I'll stay and cook." And when the brothers came home with their meat, they found a fine supper waiting.

"Has anybody been here?" Smoking Mountain asked.

"Under that robe over there." said Little-Man, pointing to a buffalo robe on the floor, "there's a large flat stone, and under the stone there's a hole. Someone lifted the stone, came out of the hole, and crept out from under the robe."

"And what happened then?" asked the brothers.

"The same thing that happened to you. An ugly dwarf, only as big as my hand but monstrously strong, tried to beat me up with his whip. So that's why you were moaning and groaning. And you were ashamed to tell because he was so small."

"Ah," said the brothers, "he whipped you too."

"No," said Little-Man, "I didn't give him the chance. I killed him and threw him down that hole."

Smoking Mountain pushed aside the robe, lifted up the stone, and peeked down. "This is a very deep hole," he said. "It must lead to that dwarf's home. I wish I could go down and find out."

Little-Man-with-Hair-All-Over said: "That's easy." He took hold of the big cooking kettle and fastened a long rawhide rope to its handle. "Climb into this kettle," he told Smoking Mountain, "and we'll let you down. Then we'll draw you up and you can tell us about it." They lowered Smoking Mountain down the hole and after a while pulled him up.

Smoking Mountain reported: "I landed right on top of that dwarf; you really fixed him good. It was dark and damp down there, and I could hear a strange noise like an animal snorting. I didn't feel comfortable in that place."

"Let me down," said Broken War Club. "I'm not afraid."

So they let him down and after a while pulled him up. He said: "I went a little farther. There's a door down there, a kind of hole in a cave wall, covered with a rock. I heard the noise too—it sounds like a deep growl rather than a snort. I didn't want to go in there."

"Let me down," said Little-Man-with-Hair-All-Over.

After they had lowered him, Little-Man found the entrance door and listened to the growling snort, or snorting growl. He rolled the rock out of the way and found himself in a cave-like room face to face with a two-headed monster. The monster growled: "Where is my son? Have you seen him? He is only so big . . . "

"That must be the dwarf I killed," said Little-Man-with-Hair-All-Over. "I left his body outside."

At this the monster roared and attacked. Little-Man managed to cut off one of its heads with his magic knife, but the monster continued fighting just as savagely. They struggled until Little-Man succeeded in cutting off the other head.

Looking past the monster's corpse, Little-Man saw another door opposite the first one. It too was stopped up with a big rock. From behind came a truly terrifying growling, snorting, and snuffling, as from a horde of strange beasts.

"I wonder who that can be," he thought, rolling the rock out of the way. In the next room he found a scaly man-monster with three heads all three of which were snorting and growling and snuffling at the same time.

"Where is my son, the one with two heads?" the monster asked.

"Grandfather—or is it grandfathers?—he is dead. I had to kill him, because otherwise, I think he would have killed me. He was mad because I killed his son—your grandson, probably—the evil little dwarf with the whip."

At this the three-headed monster hurled himself at Little-Man. The three heads foamed at the lips, snarled and bit. "One at a time, one at a time," said Little-Man as he cut the three heads off one after the other.

"They really made me sweat," said Little-Man, looking around. He discovered yet another door, behind which he heard howling, shuffling, snarling, and growling. "This is getting boring," he said as he rolled the rock aside and met a horny-skinned, four-headed man-monster. This one asked no questions but immediately jumped at Little-Man with four sets of teeth biting, snapping, and tearing. The monster's skin was so tough, especially at the necks, that it resisted the magic knife. Even when Little-Man had finally cut off three of the four heads, the man-monster fought as fiercely as ever The fourth head was the toughest; it bit a good-sized piece out of Little-Man's shoulder before he managed to cut it off. Panting, exhausted, Little-Man-with-Hair-All-Over kicked the giant body of the monster and said, "There, you wicked little thing!"

Again he looked around and saw a door. "Not again!" he said. But he listened and behind it he heard the sweet song of young girls. "This is much better," said Little-Man-with-Hair-All-Over as he rolled the last rock aside. He stepped into the last chamber and found three very pretty young women.

"Are the monsters out there relatives of yours?" asked Little-Man.

"No, no, in no way!" answered the maidens. "These horrible monsters have been keeping us prisoner for their own pleasure. We've been having a hard life."

"I believe it," he said.

"Handsome young warrior," said one of the girls, "surely you've come to free us."

"I don't know about handsome," said Little-Man, "but free you I will."

"And you are handsome," said the bold girl. "I like a little, hairy, lusty fellow."

"Then you've met the right man," he said. He looked around and saw wonderful things that the monsters had taken from their victims: buckskin robes decorated with multicolored porcupine quills, well-made weapons, war bonnets of eagle feathers, and much wore.

"Enough here for three friends to divide," said Little-Man, "and isn't it a lucky coincidence that there are three of you and three of us? For I have two friends waiting in the lodge above."

"Better and better," said the three good-looking girls.

Little-Man-with-Hair-All-Over gathered up the many fine things in a bundle and walked to the hole underneath the lodge. "Ho, friends," he hollered, "here are some good things for us to divide!" He placed the bundle in the kettle, and the two brothers in the lodge pulled it up. They called down, "Are you coming up now?"

"Not yet," he answered. "First pull up three young pretty ones well worth meeting." The brothers lowered the kettle and, one by one, drew up the women. Then Little-Man called out: "I'm coming up now." He climbed into the kettle. When they had pulled him halfway up, Broken War Club said to Smoking Mountain: "Let's drop him back down. Then we can keep these pretty girls and all the fine things for ourselves."

"No," said Smoking Mountain, "Little-Man has been a good friend to us." But Broken War Club had already cut the rawhide rope, and Little-Man fell all the way down with a big clatter. He was stunned, but recovered quickly, saying: "Some fine friends I chose!"

Without the rope and the kettle, Little-Man-with-Hair-All-Over had a hard time climbing up into the lodge. He tried four times before he finally did it. "Now I'll find these no-good brothers," he said.

Traveling along what he believed to be the trail of Smoking Mountain and Broken War Club, Little-Man heard some people quarreling. He followed the sound and came upon the body of a big elk, over which a wasp, a worm, and a woodpecker were squabbling. "My friends," Little-Man-with-Hair-All-Over told them, "there's enough here for all. Let me settle this for you and stop all the fuss." He gave the bones to the woodpecker, the fat to the wasp, and the meat to the worm, and everyone was satisfied.

"Thank you, uncle, for settling this matter and making peace between us," they said. "In return, if you ever find yourself in trouble, you can assume any of our shapes: you can turn yourself into a worm, a wasp, or a woodpecker."

"Thank you, I appreciate it," said Little-Man.

Always following the trail, he came at last to a lodge standing in a clearing of the forest. At once he turned himself into a woodpecker, flew up to a pole above the smoke hole, and looked down. "Ah," he said to himself, "Here are the two no-good brothers talking to the three girls." Then he turned himself into a wasp and flew down into the lodge, where he settled on the shoulder of the bold girl. Nobody noticed him. The bold girl said: "I'm still angry with you men. It was mean to drop that nice little fellow. He was brave, and I was fond of him. I hope he's well, wherever he is."

Smoking Mountain added, "Yes, it wasn't right. I tried to stop it, but this one here had already cut the rope."

Broken War Club just laughed. "Brother, don't talk like a fool. It was so funny, dropping that hairy, useless man down there and listening to him squeal. Look at all the riches I got for us, and look at these pretty girls who, thanks to me, make our nights pleasant. Yes, I still have to laugh when I think of the hairy one clattering down, squealing."

"I don't remember having squealed," said Little-Man-with-Hair-All Over, quickly turning himself back into a man. "Let's see who'll be squealing now."

Broken War Club tried to run away, but Little-Man seized him by the hair and cut his throat with the magic knife. Then he kicked Smoking Mountain in the backside. "Coward! You could have defied

173

your younger brother and gotten me out of that hole. If you ever cross my path again, I'll kill you the way I killed this one." Smoking Mountain slunk away.

Then Little-Man turned to the women. "Good-looking girls, will you take me for a husband? I'm man enough for three. I'm small, but not everywhere."

"Handsome one," said the bold girl, "since we three are sisters, it's only fitting for us to have one husband." So Little-Man-with-Hair-All Over married the girls, and they were all very happy together.

After Little-Man had lived with them for a while, he said: "My dears, I'm not made to stay always in one place. Now and then I just have to roam and discover things. I've left enough meat, pemmican, tongues, and back fat to last you a good many days. I won't be away for long, so don't be afraid."

Thus Little-Man-with-Hair-All-Over went traveling again. He came to a lodge, inside which a pretty young woman was crying. He went in and asked "Good-looking one, what's the matter?"

"A slimy water monster is keeping me prisoner, and I hate his embraces. I've tried and tried to run away, but he always catches me and drags me back."

"Dry your tears," said Little-Man, "I'll kill this monster and marry you. I already have three wives, but I can easily take care of one more."

"I'd like that," said the woman, "but no one can kill him."

"I can kill any monster with my magic knife. I am forever rescuing pretty maidens imprisoned by evil monsters; I'm quite used to it."

"You can't kill this one, even with a magic knife, because he's many monsters in one. There's a secret way to kill him, and if you don't happen to know it, he'll kill you."

"And what is this secret way?"

"I don't know; I've never had a chance to ask. But tonight the monster comes back, and I'll try to get it out of him. Hide yourself in the mean time."

"That's easy," said Little-Man, turning into a woodpecker and flying to the top pole above the smoke hole.

At nightfall the water monster returned. Looking down from his perch, Little-Man thought: "This is indeed an ugly, slimy monster!"

The creature threw some meat to the girl, saying: "I just drowned and ate some humans, so I'm full, but here's some antelope meat for you."

"Just what I like," said the girl. "You know, that horn coming out of your forehead is dirty; let me clean it for you. It's really quite handsome."

"You're pleasant today for a change," said the monster," instead of scowling and sour-faced. Perhaps you're beginning to appreciate me."

"How could anyone not appreciate you?" said the girl. "Tell me, so that in case of trouble I can help you: what's the only way to kill you?"

The monster grinned horribly and said: "Well, here I am, the great water monster. If you kill me, a huge grizzly bear will come out of me, and out of him a smaller brown bear, and out of him a panther, and out of the panther a wolf, and out of the wolf a wolverine, and out of that a fox, and out of that a rabbit. Out of the rabbit will come a quail, and out of the quail an egg. Only by dashing this egg against the horn in my forehead can I be killed."

Little-Man heard it all. At once he flew down into the lodge, resumed his own shape, and attacked the great water monster with his magic knife. One after the other, he killed all the animals coming out of the monster, and at last dashed the egg against the monster's horn.

"You're brave and powerful," said the girl. "I'm yours."

So Little-Man-with-Hair-All-Over took her as his fourth wife and carried her home to his lodge, together with all the treasures which the monster had amassed through robbing and murder. And Little-Man had been right: he was man enough for four wives, with a little left over.

(Quoted from Jean Desjarlais in Erdoes and Ortiz 185–91)

A particularly gruesome monster-slayer myth is this Apache version of a myth told in many parts of the world.

Jicarilla Apache: The Vagina Girls

Long ago, nearer to the beginning of this world than now, a malevolent and powerful being named Kicking Monster roamed the earth. Kicking

Monster had four daughters who were in the shape of women, but in reality they were vaginas. They were the only beings on earth who possessed vaginas, though they lived in a house—all four of them—that had vaginas hanging on the walls. But the vagina girls had legs and other body parts and could walk around.

Not surprisingly, knowledge of the vagina girls' existence spread far and wide, and many men from the Haisndayin, the people who came from below, eagerly traveled the road to their house. But when they approached, they were ambushed by Kicking Monster and kicked into the house, from which they never returned.

Then a young hero, little more than a boy, called Killer of Enemies [see the Navajo Twins] and already known for ridding the world of many monsters, heard about this alluring snare and decided to set things right. He outwitted Kicking Monster, slipping past him and entering the house, where he was set upon by the four vagina girls, who were hungry for intercourse.

Before they could lavish their attentions on him, Killer of Enemies asked them the whereabouts of all the men the monster had kicked into the house. The girls replied that they had eaten the men, which they liked to do, and they reached out lustfully for the boy.

Killer of Enemies shouted for them to stop. "Stay away from me! That's no way to use a vagina!" He knew that these four vaginas yearning for him were lined with teeth with which he too would be chewed and devoured.

He told the vagina girls that first, before any lovemaking could take place, he had to give them some medicine made of four kinds of berries. It was sour medicine, he warned them, and unlike anything they had ever tasted before, but it would make their vaginas sweet. Tantalized, the girls ate the medicine and liked it very much. Its sourness puckered up their mouths so much that they couldn't chew with their teeth and could only swallow.

The medicine not only fooled the vagina girls but destroyed their teeth altogether. So it was that the boy hero tamed the toothed vaginas so that they would thereafter always behave in a proper manner.

(Leeming, *World* 337; Opler, *Jicarilla* 66–67)

The Quest for Love

The Ojibway, or Chippewa, people tell this mysterious story of the trials of their hero Ojibwa and his quest, even into death, for his love, the Red Swan.

Ojibway: The Red Swan

There were three brothers whose father was a hermit. When the father died the brothers were orphaned and lived far off away from any other people. They managed to survive, becoming expert hunters. One day when he was out hunting, one of the brothers, called Ojibwa, noticed that the air had become reddish around him, and he heard a noise something like a human voice. He followed it to the edge of a lake, where, out in the water, he saw a red swan preening its feathers.

Ojibwa loosed an arrow at the swan, and another. The swan didn't notice, and the arrows missed. So did all the other arrows Ojibwa shot at it, until the last one penetrated the swan's neck. The bird was still, but then took wing and flew off toward the setting sun.

Ojibwa was very fleet of foot and decided to chase after the swan to retrieve his arrow. He ran all day, until just before nightfall he came to a village. The chief of the village invited Ojibwa into his lodge and, before long, offered the handsome young man his daughter as a wife.

The daughter was not pleased with this idea, and neither was Ojibwa, who resolved to leave at dawn. But he asked the daughter about the swan, and she told him she had seen it fly past and pointed out the direction.

All the next day, Ojibwa ran in that direction, and that night he came to another village where the chief offered him his daughter. Once again, Ojibwa decided to follow the swan instead, and the daughter pointed the way.

The next night, Ojibwa came across an old man living alone. This was a magician who made a kettle appear with food in it, and he fed Ojibwa. The old man explained that the red swan had passed this way many times, and those who had followed never returned. But, he said, Ojibwa would succeed if he was strong of mind.

The next night Ojibwa encountered a second old man, who fed him and explained that the red swan was the daughter of a wealthy magician who valued his daughter hardly at all. The magician had once worn a scalp of wampum, but some other Indians had asked to take it so that their chief's daughter might be cured of a mysterious sickness. Finally he had agreed and had given them the scalp, leaving his own head raw and bloody, and the Indians had never brought it back to him. His daughter, the red swan, had been enticing young men ever since to get the scalp back. Whoever succeeds, this second old man explained, will get the red swan for his wife.

The next day, Ojibwa set forth and soon enough came across a lodge from which the sounds of a man groaning could be heard. There he found the magician with the raw and bloody head. Behind a partition in the lodge came a rustling sound, and Ojibwa wondered if it might be the red swan. But before he could find out, the old magician asked to hear Ojibwa's dreams. With each telling of a dream, the old man groaned, saying "No, no," until Ojibwa told his last dream and the magician said, "Yes, you will get my scalp for me."

So again Ojibwa set forth, soon coming to another village where a lot of people were shouting and performing a war dance around a high post. On the post something was waving in the wind, and Ojibwa soon realized it was the scalp he sought. He changed into a hummingbird and flew near the scalp, but fearing he might be detected, he changed again—into a tuft of down—and floated onto the scalp. He untied it from the post and floated off, changing once again—this time into a hawk—and he carried the scalp back to the magician's house. There he put it firmly onto the old man's head, where it fit perfectly, and the old man was suddenly transformed into a handsome young man, his former self.

Ojibwa and the magician became friends and stayed there for several days. Out of courtesy Ojibwa never mentioned the red swan, and neither did the magician. On the day Ojibwa was to leave, the magician brought her forth—now she was a beautiful young woman, so beautiful she was nearly unearthly. The magician told Ojibwa to take her with him as his wife.

So Ojibwa took his new wife, the beautiful woman who had been the red swan, on his journey home to his brothers. Along the way he passed through the two villages he had visited, and the chiefs sent their daughters along with him. When Ojibwa and his bride came home, he presented the women to his brothers as their wives, and everyone lived peacefully for a long time.

But then, one time when Ojibwa had been gone on a long, long hunting trip, he came home to discover his two brothers quarreling over which one would have Ojibwa's wife. She, however, had remained constant and was mourning because she thought Ojibwa was dead, so long had he been gone.

Without saying a word, Ojibwa killed the two brothers with arrows, and he and the red swan lived on in a strong union and happy life.

(Bierhorst, *Red Swan* 277–94 from Schoolcraft)

The Savior Hero

A culture hero for the northern Cheyenne of the Great Plains is Sweet Medicine, born of a virgin and savior to his people. His story was told by the Strange Owl family on the Lame Deer Reservation.

Cheyenne: The Life and Death of Sweet Medicine

A long time ago the people had no laws, no rules of behavior—they hardly knew enough to survive. And they did shameful things out of ignorance, because they didn't understand how to live.

There was one man among them who had a natural sense of what was right. He and his wife were good, hard-working people, a family to be proud of. They knew how to feel ashamed, and this feeling kept them from doing wrong.

Their only child was a daughter, beautiful and modest, who had reached the age when girls begin to think about husbands and making a family. One night a man's voice spoke to her in a dream: "You are handsome and strong, modest and young. Therefore Sweet Root will visit you."

179

Dismissing it as just a dream, the girl went cheerfully about her chores the next day. On the following night, however, she heard the voice again: "Sweet Root is coming—woman's medicine which makes a mother's milk flow. Sweet Root is coming as a man comes courting."

The girl puzzled over the words when she awoke, but in the end shrugged her shoulders. People can't control their dreams, she thought, and the idea of a visit from a medicine root didn't make sense.

On the third night the dream recurred, and this time it was so real that a figure seemed to be standing beside the buffalo robe she slept on. He was talking to her, telling her: "Sweet Root is coming; he is very near. Soon he will be with you."

On the fourth night she heard the same voice and saw the same figure. Disturbed, she told her mother about it the next morning. "There must be something in it," she said. It's so real, and the voice is so much like a man's voice."

"No, it's just a dream," said her mother. "It doesn't mean anything."

But from that time on, the girl felt different. Something was stirring, growing within her, and after a few months her condition became obvious: she was going to have a baby. She told her parents that no man had touched her, and they believed her. But others would not be likely to, and the girl hid her condition. When she felt the birth pangs coming on, she went out into the prairie far from the camp and built herself a brush shelter. Doing everything herself, she gave birth to a baby boy. She dried the baby, wrapped him in soft moss, and left him there in the wickiup, for in her village a baby without a father would be scorned and treated badly. Praying that someone would find him, she went sadly home to her parents.

At about the same time, an old woman was out searching the prairie for wild turnips, which she dug up with an animal's shoulder blade. She heard crying, and following the sound, came to the wickiup. She was overjoyed to find the baby, as she had never had one of her own. All around the brush shelter grew the sweet root which makes a mother's milk flow, so she named the boy Sweet Medicine. She took him home to her shabby tipi even though she had nothing to offer him but love.

In the tipi next to the old woman's lived a young mother who was nursing a small child, and she agreed to nurse Sweet Medicine also. He grew faster and learned faster than ordinary children and was weaned in no time. When he was only ten years old, he already had grown-up wisdom and hunting skill far in advance of his age. But because he had no family and lived at the edge of the camp in a poor tipi, nobody paid any attention to Sweet Medicine's exceptional powers.

That year there was a drought, very little game, and much hunger in the village. "Grandmother," Sweet Medicine said to the old woman, "find me an old buffalo hide—any dried-out, chewed-up scrap with holes in it will do."

The woman searched among the refuse piles and found a wrinkled, brittle piece that the starving dogs had been chewing on. When she brought it to Sweet Medicine, he told her, "Take this to the stream outside the camp, wash it in the flowing water, make it pliable, scrape it clean." After she had done this Sweet Medicine took a willow wand and bent it into a hoop, which he colored with sacred red earth paint. He cut the buffalo hide into one long strip and wove it back and forth over the hoop, making a kind of net with an opening in the center. Then he cut four wild cherry sticks, sharpened them to a point, and hardened them in the hearth fire.

The next morning he said: "Grandmother, come with me. We're going to play the hoop-and-stick game." He took the hoop and the cherry-wood sticks and walked into the middle of the camp circle "Grandmother, roll this hoop for me," he said. She rolled the hoop along the ground and Sweet Medicine hurled his pointed sticks through the center of it, hitting the right spot every time. Soon a lot of people, men and women, boys and girls, came to watch the strange new game.

Then Sweet Medicine cried: "Grandmother, let me hit it once more and make the hoop into a fat buffalo calf!"

Again he threw his stick like a dart, again the stick went through the center of the hoop, and as it did so the hoop turned into a fat, yellow buffalo calf. The stick had pierced its heart, and the calf fell down dead. "Now you people will have plenty to eat," said Sweet Medicine. "Come and butcher this calf."

181

The people gathered and roasted chunks of tender calf meat over their fires. And no matter how many pieces of flesh they cut from the calf's body, it was never picked clean. However much they ate, there was always more. So the people had their fill, and that was the end of the famine. It was also the first hoop-and-stick game played among the Cheyenne. This sacred game has much power attached to it, and it is still being played.

A boy's first kill is an important happening in his life, something he will always remember. After killing his first buffalo a boy will be honored by his father, who may hold a feast for him and give him a man's name. There would be no feast for Sweet Medicine; all the same, he was very happy when he killed a fat, yellow buffalo calf on his first hunt. He was skinning and butchering it when he was approached by an elderly man, a chief too old to do much hunting, but still harsh and commanding. "This is just the kind of hide I have been looking for," said the chief. "I will take it."

"You can't have a boy's first hide," said Sweet Medicine. "Surely you must know this. But you are welcome to half of the meat, because I honor old age."

The chief took the meat but grabbed the hide too and began to walk off with it. Sweet Medicine took hold of one end, and they started a tug-of-war. The chief used his riding whip on Sweet Medicine, shouting: "How dare a poor nothing boy defy a chief?" As he whipped Sweet Medicine again and again across the face, the boy's fighting spirit was aroused. He grabbed a big buffalo leg bone and hit the old man over the head.

Some say Sweet Medicine killed that chief, others say the old man just fell down stunned. But in the village the people were angry that a mere boy had dared to fight the old chief. Some said, "Let's whip him," others said, "Let's kill him."

After he had returned to the old woman's lodge, Sweet Medicine sensed what was going on. He said: "Grandmother, some young men of the warrior societies will come here to kill me for having stood up for myself." He thanked her for her kindness to him and then fled from the village. Later when the young warriors came, they were so angry to find the boy gone that they pulled the lodge down and set fire to it.

The following morning someone saw Sweet Medicine, dressed like a Fox warrior, standing on a hill overlooking the village. His enemies set out in pursuit, but he was always just out of their reach and they finally retired exhausted. The next morning he appeared as an Elk warrior, carrying a crooked coupstick wrapped in otter skin. Again they tried to catch and kill him, and again he evaded them. They resumed their futile chase on the third morning, when he wore the red face paint and feathers of a Red Shield warrior, and on the fourth, when he dressed like a Dog soldier and shook a small red rattle tied with buffalo hair at his pursuers. On the fifth day he appeared in the full regalia of a Cheyenne chief. That made the village warriors angrier than ever, but they still couldn't catch him, and after that they saw him no more.

Wandering alone over the prairie, the boy heard a voice calling, leading him to a beautiful dark-forested land of many hills. Standing apart from the others was a single mountain shaped like a huge tipi: the sacred medicine mountain called Bear Butte. Sweet Medicine found a secret opening which has since closed (or perhaps was visible to him alone) and entered the mountain. It was hollow inside like a tipi, forming a sacred lodge filled with people who looked like ordinary men and women, but were really powerful spirits.

"Grandson, come in, we have been expecting you," the holy people said, and when Sweet Medicine took his seat, they began teaching him the Cheyenne way to live so that he could return to the people and give them this knowledge.

First of all, the spirits gave him the sacred four arrows, saying: "This is the great gift we are handing you. With these wonderful arrows, the tribe will prosper. Two arrows are for war and two for hunting. But there is much, much more to the four arrows. They have great powers. They contain rules by which men ought to live."

The spirit people taught Sweet Medicine how to pray to the arrows, how to keep them, how to renew them. They taught him the wise laws of the forty-four chiefs. They taught him how to set up rules for the warrior societies. They taught him how women should be honored. They taught him the many useful things by which people could live, survive, and

183

prosper, things·people had not yet learned at that time. Finally they taught him how to make a special tipi in which the sacred arrows were to be kept. Sweet Medicine listened respectfully and learned well, and finally an old spirit man burned incense of sweet grass to purify both Sweet Medicine and the sacred arrow bundle. Then the Cheyenne boy put the holy bundle on his back and began the long journey home to his people.

During his absence there had been a famine in the land. The buffalo had gone into hiding, for they were angry that the people did not know how to live and were behaving badly. When Sweet Medicine arrived at the village, he found a group of tired and listless children, their ribs sticking out, who were playing with little buffalo figures they had made out of mud. Sweet Medicine immediately changed the figures into large chunks of juicy buffalo meat and fat. "Now there's enough for you to eat," he told the young ones, "with plenty left over for your parents and grandparents. Take the meat, fat, and tongues into the village, and tell two good young hunters to come out in the morning to meet me."

Though the children carried the message and two young hunters went out and looked everywhere for Sweet Medicine the next day, all they saw was a big eagle circling above them. They tried again on the second and third days with no success, but on the fourth morning they found Sweet Medicine standing on top of a hill overlooking the village. He told the two: "I have come bringing a wonderful gift from the Creator which the spirits inside the great medicine mountain have sent you. Tell the people to set up a big lodge in the center of the camp circle. Cover its floor with sage, and purify it with burning sweet grass. Tell everyone to go inside the tipi and stay there; no one must see me approaching."

When at last all was ready, Sweet Medicine walked slowly toward the village and four times called out: "People of the Cheyenne, with a great power I am approaching. Be joyful. The sacred arrows I am bringing." He entered the tipi with the sacred arrow bundle and said: "You have not yet learned how to live in the right way. That is why the Ones Above were angry and the buffalo went into hiding." The two young hunters lit the fire, and Sweet Medicine filled a deer-bone pipe with sacred tobacco. All night through, he taught the people what the spirits inside the holy mountain had taught him. These teachings established the way of the Tsistsistas, the true Cheyenne nation. Toward morning Sweet Medicine sang four sacred songs. After each song he smoked the pipe, and its holy breath ascended through the smoke hole up into the sky, up to the great mystery.

At daybreak, as the sun rose and the people emerged from the sacred arrow lodge, they found the prairie around them covered with buffalo. The spirits were no longer angry. The famine was over.

For many nights to come, Sweet Medicine instructed the people in the sacred laws. He lived among the Cheyenne for a long time and made them into a proud tribe respected throughout the Plains.

Four lives the Creator had given him, but even Sweet Medicine was not immortal. Only the rocks and mountains are forever. When he grew old and feeble and felt that the end of his appointed time was near, he directed the people to carry him to a place near the Sacred Bear Butte. There they made a small hut for him out of cottonwood branches and cedar lodge poles covered with bark and leaves. They spread its floor with sage, flat cedar leaves, and fragrant grass. It was a good lodge to die in, and when they placed him before it, he addressed the people for the last time:

> I have seen in my mind that some time after I am dead—and may the time be long—light-skinned, bearded men will arrive with sticks spitting fire. They will conquer the land and drive you before them. They will kill the animals who give their flesh that you may live, and they will bring strange animals for you to ride and eat. They will introduce war and evil, strange sicknesses and death. They will try to make you forget Maheo, the Creator, and the things I taught you, and will impose their own alien, evil ways. They will take your land little by little until there is nothing left for you. I do not like to tell you this, but you must know. You must be strong when that bad time comes, you men, and particularly you women, because much depends on you, because you are the

perpetuators of life and if you weaken, the Cheyenne will cease to be. Now I have said all there is to say.

Then Sweet Medicine went into his hut to die.
(Quoted from the Strange Owl Family in Erdoes and Ortiz 199–205)

Heroines

As has been noted, myths of heroism are usually derived from warrior and hunting activities commonly associated with males. The relatively few heroines in Indian mythology usually stand out in connection with some practice or activity associated with women in the culture, or they take on a role usually played by men.

The Heroine and the Family

The Tlingit of British Columbia are perhaps best known for their totem poles. These poles are, in fact, crest poles that celebrate the symbols relating to a particular family—rather like a coat of arms in Europe. Since the Tlingits are matrilineal, the myths that lie behind the symbolism of the poles—the crest myths—are often about heroines rather than heroes. This tale, which "explains" the woodworm as a family crest figure, is an example.

Tlingit: The Woodworm

A chief's daughter was secretly keeping a pet woodworm, and she fed it oils of different kinds until it was as long as a man's arms stretched out to the side. She used to sing lullabies to it, and people heard her singing. She kept the woodworm in her room and came out herself only to eat. No one knew she was raising a woodworm in there.

One day her mother spied on her and saw something horrible in her room. But the girl seemed to be happy with it, so her mother didn't say anything. Around this time, the people of the town began to be missing oil. The worm, you see, was stealing it from them. So the mother told her daughter that maybe she should have a different pet. The girl only cried, saying that the worm was her son.

Finally the people decided they had better kill the worm, and they told the girl to bring it out to them. She refused, but finally gave in and brought the worm out, singing a song about it. Soon, when she was told that her son was dead, she sang another song that said, "I am blamed for bringing you up, but one day you will be claimed by a great clan." And since then the Ganatedi clan, whenever they have a feast, sings the songs the woman made up, and the woodworm is one of their crests.

(Bierhorst, Mythology 41–44 from Swanton)

The Heroine as Savior

There are times when the woman plays the typically male role of warrior. Some such myths develop from historical or legendary events. One such myth is told by the Oneida, one of the Iroquois nations. The heroine is the maiden Aliquispo, whose self-sacrifice saved her people.

Oneida: Aliquispo, Brave Woman

In the old days before the coming of the white man, the Oneida people had their traditional enemies, the Mingo, who invaded their villages, burned their houses and fields, killed the men and boys, and took away the women and girls. In one such raid the Mingo were too numerous to resist, so the Oneida who managed to escape hid in a high cave in the forest, where they were protected by the Great Spirit. But the people were starving; they had to either die in their hiding place or search for food and thus attract the attention of their enemies.

During the great council that was held to decide what to do, a young woman called Aliquispo came forward and announced that the spirits had spoken to her in a vision and had told her that her destiny was to save the people. "Stay here in the cliff cave," she told the Oneida, "while I go to the Mingo and lead them to the space below. Then you will be able to crush them." The elders all praised Aliquispo for her bravery and for understanding the role given to her by the Great Spirit.

The girl made her way to the old Oneida village where the Mingo now lived. As she knew they would, the Mingo threatened to burn her alive if she did not lead them to her people. So that the enemies would not be suspicious, Aliquispo refused and was immediately tied to a stake. After enduring the torture of the hot flames for an amazingly long time, she pretended to give in and, with her hands tied behind her back, she led the Mingo during the night to the space below the cliff hiding place. She whispered to the Mingo that they should gather close to her so that she could tell them of the secret path that would lead to her sleeping friends and relatives. As soon as the enemies were massed around her she cried out in a loud voice, "My people, your enemies are here; destroy them." The Mingo struck her down, but were themselves struck down by a huge rain of boulders and rocks thrown from the hiding place above.

So it was that Aliquispo died to save her people forever from the Mingo. To honor her, the Great Spirit turned her hair into woodbine and made honeysuckle grow from her body. Woodbine is fine medicine, and honeysuckle is called by the Oneida "brave women's blood."

(Erdoes and Ortiz 252–53 from Canfield)

Makhta, or Brave Woman, of the White Water Sioux was also a savior heroine, an Indian Joan of Arc.

Sioux: Makhta, Brave Woman

A great chief had three sons and a daughter. The sons wanted to earn greatness as warriors just as their father had, and they all took part in fighting against the Crow Indians, but eventually each one was killed in battle. Now the old chief had but one child left, his daughter, who some say was named Makhta, or Brave Woman.

She was a beautiful young woman and many young men sent their fathers to ask that she be their bride. But she always refused to marry, saying instead that she wanted to avenge her dead brothers. One of these suitors was Red Horn, the son of another chief, and another was Little Eagle, who was too shy to ask, being a poor boy.

Around this time, the Crow began to invade Sioux country again and it was decided that a war party should be sent out to fight them. Makhta begged her father to let her go with them. The old man told her he feared she would be killed and he didn't want to live out his days with no children at all, but he realized she had already made up her mind. He gave Makhta her brothers' weapons and his own war bonnet to wear, and she rode out with the warriors. She gave the weapons to the others, including Little Eagle and Red Horn, keeping only her father's well-worn old coup stick.

Soon the Sioux party came across a huge Crow encampment and, even though they were greatly outnumbered, they attacked it. Makhta hung back, singing the war songs and making the trilling noise women make to encourage their men in war. Soon the Sioux were driven back, and she rode into the midst of the enemy. She didn't try to kill, only to count coup, touching the Crow with her coup stick here and there, this one and that one. She showed such bravery that the warriors fought again.

But again they were driven back, and Makhta's horse was struck by a musket ball. Little Eagle rode toward her, dismounted, and told her to get on his horse. She did, expecting him to leap up behind her, but he said the horse had been wounded and was too weak to carry two.

"I won't leave you to be killed," she cried, but he slapped the horse on the rump and it bolted away. Little Eagle went back into battle on foot, and Makhta, on his horse, rallied the warriors for one more assault, which was so furious that it drove the teeming Crows back and away for good.

But many young Sioux had been killed, including Little Eagle. His comrades had placed his body on a high scaffold and killed his horse so that it would go with him in the land of many lodges.

Hearing of this, Makhta cut her arms and legs, and tore her dress, and mourned for Little Eagle as though he had been her husband. She never

189

ceased mourning for him, never took a husband, and died of old age, famous still for her great deeds.

(Erdoes and Ortiz 258–60 from Jenny Leading Cloud)

All of these heroes and heroines are marked by their super-human or near-superhuman abilities, but in the dream that is Native American mythology they represent the human element. In a world seething with spirits who would help and monsters who would destroy the human race, the Indian heroes on their quests, like their counterparts in other parts of the world, are metaphors for the drive for survival and identity that motivates us all. In fact, if one dominant message emerges from the complexity that is North American Indian mythology, it is that our surroundings, both animate and inanimate, are literally alive with the power of a great mystery and that human survival depends on our having the vision, the patience, and the willingness to receive that power. In the Indian myth-dream we humans are helped on our quest by culture heroes, tricksters, and lesser heroes, all of whom represent our ability, when we are in tune with reality, to overcome the impossible and to fulfill our destinies.

Bibliography

This bibliography contains works cited as well as works of general and specific interest to the student of American Indian mythology. Books particularly useful as source material for this volume are marked with an asterisk. The primary source for myths quoted directly from Native American storytellers is *American Indian Myths and Legends*, by Richard Erdoes and Alfonso Ortiz, which is by far the most comprehensive collection of Indian myths available.

Allen, Paula Gunn. *Grandmothers of the Light: A Medicine Woman's Sourcebook.* Boston: Beacon Press, 1991.

Anderson, F. G. "The Pueblo Kachina Cult: A Historical Reconstruction." *Southwestern Journal of Anthropology* 11, 404–19.

Bagley, C. B. *Indian Myths of the Northwest.* Seattle: Lowman and Hanford, 1930.

Bahti, Tom. *Southwestern Indian Ceremonials.* Flagstaff: KC Publications, 1971.

Beckwith, Martha Warren. *Mandan-Hitatsu Myths and Ceremonies.* Memoirs of the American Folklore Society, 1938. New York: American Folklore Society, 1937.

Benedict, Ruth. *Patterns of Culture.* 1934. New York: New American Library, 1959.

———. "Serrano Tales." *Journal of American Folklore* 39 (1926): 8.

———. *Zuni Mythology.* Columbia University Contributions to Anthropology, vol. 21. New York: Columbia University Press, 1935.

*Bierhorst, John. *The Mythology of North America*. New York: Morrow, 1985.

*———. *The Red Swan: Myths and Tales of the American Indians*. New York: Farrar, Straus, and Giroux, 1976.

Bierlein, J. F. *Parallel Myths*. New York: Ballantine Books, 1994.

Binford, Sally. "Myths and Matriarchies." *Anthropology 81/82* 1 (1981): 150–53.

Boas, Franz. *Chinook Texts*. Bureau of American Ethnology Bulletin 20. Washington, D.C.: Government Printing Office, 1894.

*———. *Keresan Texts*. New York: Publications of the American Ethnological Society, 1928.

———. *Tsimshian Mythology*. Bureau of American Ethnology Bulletin 27. Washington, D.C.: Government Printing Office, 1902.

Brandon, William. *The Last Americans: The Indian in American Culture*. New York: McGraw-Hill, 1974.

Bright, William. *The Coyote Reader*. Berkeley: University of California Press, 1993.

Brown, Charles E. *Wigwam Tales*. Madison: University of Wisconsin Press, 1930.

Brown, Dee. *Folktales of Native America*. New York: Holt, Rinehart, and Winston, 1979.

Brown, Joseph Epes. *The Sacred Pipe: Black Elk's Account of the Seven Rites of the Oglala Sioux*. Norman: University of Oklahoma Press, 1953.

———. *The Spiritual Legacy of the American Indian*. New York: Crossroads Publishing Co., 1989.

Bullchild, Percy. *The Sun Came Down: The History of the World as My Blackfeet Elders Told It*. San Francisco: Harper and Row, 1985.

Campbell, Joseph. *The Flight of the Wild Gander*. 1951. New York: HarperCollins, 1990.

———. *The Hero with a Thousand Faces*. 1959. Princeton: Princeton University Press, 1968.

———. *The Masks of God*. 4 vols. New York: Viking, 1970.

————. *The Way of the Animal Powers.* San Francisco: Harper and Row, 1983.

*Canfield, W. W. *The Legends of the Iroquois, "Told by the Cornplanter."* New York: A. Wessels, 1902.

Capps, Walter H., and Åke Hultkrantz, eds. *Seeing with a Native Eye.* New York: Harper and Row, 1976.

Catlin, George. *North American Indians.* London: George Catlin, 1841, 1856.

*Clark, Ella. *Indian Legends from the Northern Rockies.* Norman: University of Oklahoma Press, 1966.

*————. *Indian Legends of the Pacific Northwest.* Berkeley: University of California Press, 1953.

Coffin, T. P. *Indian Tales of North America.* Philadelphia: American Folklore Society, 1961.

*Cornplanter, Jesse J. *Legends of the Longhouse.* Philadelphia: Lippincott, 1938.

Courlander, Harold. *The Fourth World of the Hopi.* New York: Crown Publishers, 1971.

Croyn, George W., ed. *American Indian Poetry: An Anthology of Songs and Chants.* New York: Liveright, 1934.

Cunningham, Keith. *American Indians' Kitchen-Table Stories.* Little Rock: August House, 1992.

Curry, J. L. *Back in the Beforetime: Tales of the California Indians.* New York: M. K. McElderry Books, 1987.

Curtin, Jeremiah. *Creation Myths of Primitive America: In Relation to the Religious History and Mental Development of Mankind.* Boston: Little, Brown, 1898.

Curtis, Edward S. *The North American Indian.* Cambridge, Mass.: The University Press, 1924.

Curtis, Natalie. *The Indians' Book.* 1907. New York: Harper, 1968.

*Cushing, Frank H. "Outlines of Zuni Creation Myths." In *Thirteenth Annual Report of the Bureau of American Ethnology . . . 1891–1892,* 321-447. Washington, D.C.: Government Printing Office, 1896.

Deloria, Vine, Jr. *God Is Red: A Native View of Religion.* 1973. Golden, Colo.: North American Press, 1992.

DeMallie, R. J., and D. R. Parks, eds. *Sioux Indian Religion: Tradition and Innovation.* Norman: University of Oklahoma Press, 1987.

Dixon, Richard B. "Maidu Myths." *Bulletin of the American Museum of Natural History* (New York), 17, no. 39 (1905).

Dooling, D. M., and Paul Jordan-Smith, eds. *I Become Part of It: Sacred Dimensions in Native American Life.* New York: HarperCollins, 1992.

Dorsey, George A. *The Cheyenne.* Field Columbian Museum Publications in Anthropology, no. 99. Chicago: Field Museum, 1905.

Driver, H. E. *Indians of North America.* Chicago: University of Chicago Press, 1969.

DuBois, Constance G. "The Mythology of the Diegueños." *Journal of American Folklore* 14 (1901): 181–82.

Dundes, Alan A., ed. *The Flood Myth.* Berkeley: University of California Press, 1988.

Edmonds, Margot, and Ella E. Clark. *Voices of the Winds: Native American Legends.* New York: Facts on File, 1989.

Eliade, Mircea. *The Encyclopedia of Religion.* 16 vols. New York: Macmillan, 1987. (Especially important are the Native American articles in volume 10.)

———. *The Myth of the Eternal Return.* 1954. Princeton: Princeton University Press, 1974.

———. *Patterns in Comparative Religion.* 1958. Cleveland: World Publishing Co., 1966.

———. *Shamanism: Archaic Techniques of Ecstasy.* 1964. Princeton: Princeton University Press, 1972.

*Erdoes, Richard, and Alfonso Ortiz, eds. *American Indian Myths and Legends.* New York: Pantheon, 1984.

Farmer, Penelope, ed. *Beginnings: Creation Myths of the World.* New York: Atheneum, 1979.

Forde, Daryll C. *Folklore* 41. London: William Glaisher, 1930.

Gill, Sam D. *Native American Religions: An Introduction.* Belmont, Calif.: Wadsworth Publishing Co., 1981.

*Gill, Sam D., and Irene F. Sullivan. *Dictionary of Native American Mythology.* New York: Oxford University Press, 1994.

Goddard, Pliny Earle. "Hupa Texts." *University of California Publications in American Archeology and Ethnology* 1 (1904): 84–368.

*Grinnell, George Bird. *Blackfoot Lodge Tales.* 1892. Lincoln: University of Nebraska, 1962.

———. *The Cheyenne Indians.* 1923. 2 vols. Lincoln: University of Nebraska Press, 1972.

Hamilton, Virginia. *In the Beginning: Creation Stories from around the World.* New York: Harcourt, 1988.

Hewitt, J. N. B. "Iroquoian Cosmology." Part 1. *Twenty-first Annual Report of the Bureau of American Ethnology . . . 1899–1900,* 127-339. Washington, D.C.: Government Printing Office, 1903.

———. "Iroquoian Cosmology." Part 2. *Forty-third Annual Report of the Bureau of American Ethnology . . . 1925–1926,* 449–819. Washington, D.C.: Government Printing Office, 1928.

Hoffman, Walter J. "The Menomini Indians." *Fourteenth Annual Report of the Bureau of American Ethnology,* 3–328. Washington, D.C.: Government Printing Office, 1896.

Hudson, Charles. *The Southeastern Indians.* Knoxville: University of Tennessee Press, 1976.

Hultkrantz, Åke. *The North American Indian Orpheus Tradition.* Stockholm: Ethnographical Museum of Sweden, 1957.

———. *The Religions of the American Indians.* Berkeley: University of California Press, 1979.

———. *The Study of American Indian Religions.* New York: Crossroad Publishing, 1983.

Johnson, Frederick, ed. *Man in Northeastern North America.* Papers of the Robert S. Peabody Foundation for Archeology, vol. 3. Andover, Mass., 1946.

Johnston, Basil. *The Manitous: The Spiritual World of the Ojibway.* New York: HarperCollins, 1995.

Jung, Carl G. *Four Archetypes: Mother, Rebirth, Spirit, Trickster.* 1959. Princeton: Princeton University Press, 1970.

Kroeber, A. L. "Indian Myths of South Central California." *University of California Publications in American Archeology and Ethnology* 4, no. 4 (1906–7): 229–31.

Kroeber, Karl, ed. *Traditional Literatures of the American Indians.* Lincoln: University of Nebraska Press, 1981.

Lankford, G. E., III, ed. *Native American Legends: Southeastern Legends.* Little Rock: August House, 1987.

LaPointe, James. *Legends of the Lakota.* San Francisco: Indian Historian Press, 1976.

Leach, Maria. *The Beginning: Creation Myths around the World.* New York: Thomas Y. Crowell, 1956.

*Leeming, David A. *Mythology: The Voyage of the Hero.* 1973. New York: Harper and Row, 1981.

*———. *The World of Myth.* New York: Oxford University Press, 1990.

*Leeming, David A., and Margaret A. Leeming. *A Dictionary of Creation Myths.* 1994. New York: Oxford University Press, 1995.

*Leeming, David A., and Jake Page. *God: Myths of the Male Divine.* New York: Oxford University Press, 1996.

*———. *Goddess: Myths of the Female Divine.* New York: Oxford University Press, 1994.

Leland, Charles. *Algonquin Legends of New England.* Boston: Houghton Mifflin, 1884.

Levi-Strauss, Claude. "The Structural Study of Myth." *Journal of American Folklore* 68 (1955): 428–44.

Locke, Raymond Friday. *The Book of the Navajo.* Los Angeles: Mankind, 1976.

*Long, Charles H. *Alpha: The Myths of Creation.* New York: George Braziller, 1963.

*Marriott, Alice, and Carol K. Rachlin, eds. *American Indian Mythology.* New York: Mentor, 1968.

*————. *Plains Indian Mythology.* New York: Mentor, 1975.

Mason, J. A. "The Language of the Salinan Indians." *University of California Publications in American Archeology and Ethnology* 14, no. 1 (1918).

Miller, Jay. *Earthmaker: Tribal Stories from Native North America.* New York: Putnam, 1992.

*Momaday, N. Scott. *The Way to Rainy Mountain.* Albuquerque: University of New Mexico Press, 1969.

Mooney, James. "The Jicarilla Genesis." *American Anthropologist* 11 (1898): 197–200.

*————. *Myths of the Cherokee. Nineteenth Annual Report of the Bureau of American Ethnology . . . 1897–1898.* Washington, D.C.: Government Printing Office, 1902).

Mourning Dove. *Coyote Stories.* Lincoln: University of Nebraska Press, 1990.

*Mullett, G. M. *Spider Woman Stories: Legends of the Hopi Indians.* Tucson: University of Arizona Press, 1982.

Neihardt, John G. *Black Elk Speaks.* 1932. Lincoln: University of Nebraska Press, 1988.

Nicolar, Joseph. *The Life and Traditions of the Red Man.* Bangor, Me.: C. H. Glass, 1893.

Olcott, William T. *Myths of the Sun.* New York: Capricorn Books, 1914.

*Opler, Morris Edward. *Myths of the Chiricahua Apache Indians. Memoirs of the American Folklore Society* (New York), 37 (1942): 1–2.

*————. *Myths and Tales of the Jicarilla Apaches.* 1938. New York: Dover, 1994.

Ortiz, Alfonso. *The Tewa World.* Chicago: University of Chicago Press, 1969.

Ostreicher, David M. "Unmasking the *Walum Olum*: A 19th-Century Hoax." *Bulletin of the Archeological Society of New Jersey* 49 (1994): 1–44.

*Page, Susanne, and Jake Page. *Hopi.* New York: Abrams, 1982.

*————. *Navajo.* New York: Abrams, 1995.

Powers, William K. *Indians of the Northern Plains.* New York: Putnam, 1969.

Radin, Paul. *The Trickster: A Study in American Indian Mythology.* 1956. New York: Schocken, 1972.

Reichard, Gladys A. "Literary Types and Dissemination of Myths." *Journal of American Folklore* 34 (1921): 269–307.

———. "Wyot Grammar and Texts." *University of California Publications in American Archeology and Ethnology* 22 (1925), no. 1.

Ridington, Robin. *Swan People: A Study of the Dunne-za Prophet Dance.* Papers of the Canadian Ethnology Service, 38. Ottawa, 1978.

Rothenberg, Jerome, ed. *Shaking the Pumpkin: Traditional Poetry of the Indian North Americas.* Garden City, N.Y.: Doubleday, 1972.

Sanders, Thomas E., and Walter W. Peek, eds. *Literature of the American Indian.* New York: Glencoe Press, 1973.

Schoolcraft, H. R. *Algic Researches.* 2 vols. New York, 1839.

———. *The Myth of Hiawatha and Other Oral Legends Mythologic and Allegoric of the North American Indians.* Philadelphia: Lippincott, 1856.

*Silko, Leslie. *Ceremony.* New York: Viking, 1978.

Smith, Erminnie. "Myths of the Iroquois." *Second Annual Report of the Bureau of American Ethnology . . . 1880–1881,* 47–116. Washington, D.C.: Government Printing Office, 1883.

*Spence, Lewis. *The Myths of the North American Indians.* 1914. New York: Dover, 1989.

*Sproul, Barbara C. *Primal Myths: Creation Myths around the World* 1979. San Francisco: HarperCollins, 1991.

Stevenson, M. C. "The Sia." *Eleventh Annual Report of the Bureau of American Ethnology . . . 1889–1890,* 3–157. Washington, D.C.: Goverment Printing Office, 1894.

Sturtevant, William C., ed. *Handbook of North American Indians.* Washington, D.C.: Smithsonian Institution, 1978–.

Swanton, John R. "Creek Stories." In *Myths and Tales of the South-eastern Indians*, p. 84. Bureau of American Ethnology Bulletin 88. Washington, D.C.: Government Printing Office, 1929.

Tedlock, Dennis, and Barbara Tedlock, eds. *Teachings from the American Earth*. New York: Liveright, 1975.

Teit, James. *Folk-Tales of the Salishan and Sahaptin Tribes*. Memoirs of the American Folklore Society, 2, p. 84. New York, 1917.

Terrell, John Upton. *Pueblos, Gods and Spaniards*. New York: Dial, 1973.

Thompson, Stith. *Motif-Index of Folk Literature*. Bloomington: Indiana University Press, 1955–58.

*———. *Tales of the North American Indians*. 1929. Bloomington: Indiana University Press, 1971.

Tooker, Elizabeth. *Native North American Spirituality of the Eastern Woodlands*. New York: Paulist Press, 1979.

*Tyler, Hamilton A. *Pueblo Gods and Myths*. Norman: University of Oklahoma Press, 1964.

Underhill, Ruth. *Papago Woman*. 1936. New York: Holt, Rinehart, and Winston, 1979.

———. *The Red Man's Religion*. Chicago: University of Chicago Press, 1965.

Utley, Francis Lee. "The Migration of Folktales: Four Channels to the Americas." *Current Anthropology* 15 (1974): 5–27.

Vecsey, Christopher. *Imagine Ourselves Richly: Mythic Narratives of North American Indians*. New York: Crossroad Publishing Co., 1988.

Voeglin, Charles, trans. *Walum Olum*. Indianapolis: Indiana Historical Society, 1954.

Voth, Henry. *The Traditions of the Hopi*. Field Columbian Museum Publications in Anthropology, 8. Chicago: Field Museum, 1905.

*Waters, Frank. *Book of the Hopi*. New York: Viking Press, 1963.

Waugh, Earle H., and K. Dad Prithipaul, eds. *Native Religious Traditions*. Waterloo, Ont.: Wilfred Laurier University Press, 1979.

*Weigle, Marta. *Creation and Procreation: Feminist Reflections on Mythologies of Cosmogony and Parturition.* Philadelphia: University of Pennsylvania Press, 1989.

Williamson, Ray A. *Living the Sky: The Cosmos of the American Indian.* Reprint. Norman: University of Oklahoma Press, 1984.

Williamson, Ray A., and Claire R. Farrer, eds. *Earth and Sky: Visions of the Cosmos in Native American Folklore.* Albuquerque: University of New Mexico Press, 1992.

Wortmington, H. M. *Ancient Man in North America.* Denver: Denver Museum of Natural History, 1957.

Wyman, Leland C. *Blessingway.* Tucson: University of Arizona Press, 1970.

Ywahoo, Dhyani. *Voices of Our Ancestors: Cherokee Teaching from the Wisdom Fire.* Boston: Shambhala, 1987.

*Zolbrod, Paul G. *Dine Bahane: The Navajo Creation Story.* Albuquerque: University of New Mexico Press, 1984.

Index